Salaam, Love

American Muslim Men on Love, Sex, and Intimacy

**Edited by Ayesha Mattu
and Nura Maznavi**

Beacon Press
Boston

Beacon Press
www.beacon.org

Beacon Press books
are published under the auspices of
the Unitarian Universalist Association of Congregations.

17 16 15 14   8 7 6 5 4 3 2 1

This book is printed on acid-free paper that meets the uncoated paper ANSI/
NISO specifications for permanence as revised in 1992.

Some names and identifying characteristics of people mentioned in this
work have been changed to protect their identities.

Text design by Ruth Maassen

In the essays "The Promise," by Alan Howard, and "Fertile Ground," by
Khizer Husain, the authors have cited Muhammad Asad's translation of the
Qur'an, *The Message of the Qur'an* (London: The Book Foundation, revised
ed., 2008).

Library of Congress Cataloging-in-Publication Data
Salaam, love : American Muslim men on love, sex, and intimacy / [edited by]
Ayesha Mattu, Nura Maznavi.
    pages cm
    ISBN 978-0-8070-7975-1 (pbk.)—ISBN 978-0-8070-7976-8 (electronic) 1.
Muslim men—United States. 2. Intimacy (Psychology)—Religious aspects—
Islam. 3. Sex role—Religious aspects—Islam. I. Mattu, Ayesha. II. Maznavi,
Nura.
  HQ1090.3.S25 2014
  305.31088'297—dc23
                        2013035892

For all the men who asked, "Where are our stories?"

Contents

Introduction

Men don't talk about their feelings—isn't that the conventional wisdom?

It's what we bought into, anyway, which is why, for a long time, we never seriously considered doing this book.

When *Love, InshAllah: The Secret Love Lives of American Muslim Women* was published two years ago—a collection in which twenty-five women raised their voices to tell their funny, romantic, and moving tales about the search for love—it resonated with countless readers around the world. Including men. They started to ask us, "Where are our stories?"

We dismissed the inquiries with a laugh. "Please! Guys don't talk about this stuff."

But as the requests kept coming—over e-mail, at book readings, even at dinner parties—it struck us: what if it's not that men don't want to talk about their feelings, but rather that they don't have the space to do so?

Men without space? It sounds absurd. After all, men dominate corner offices and the upper echelons of leadership and power, men get the best prayer space in the mosque, and men even take up the most space on the bus (dudes, put your legs together, we get it).

But what about the emotional space to be honest and vulnerable about matters of the heart, without jeopardizing notions of masculinity and manhood? The space to talk about sex, coupled with love and intimacy, without it being a joke or the raunchy punch line from a movie?

We decided to ask. After all, there are two (or more!) sides to every story.

We asked American Muslim men—our cultural and religious community—to tell us: What does it mean to be a man? To love well? To be faithful and constant? What do you do if you fail at love? How do you move forward after you've broken someone's heart, or had yours broken?

And they told us.

Stories poured in from men of diverse ethnic, racial, and religious perspectives—including orthodox, cultural, and secular Muslims. They came from single, divorced, married, and widowed men, young and old, in large cities and small towns across the country.

They told stories of love and heartbreak, loyalty and betrayal, intimacy and insecurity. And, above all else: *feelings*

In this book, we share twenty-two of them.

The title of this collection, *Salaam, Love,* couples two essential traits of the Muslim men we know: peace and love. Colloquially, *salaam* also means "hello." The men in this book greet us and welcome us—with open arms—into the most intimate aspects of their lives.

The subtitle, *American Muslim Men on Love, Sex, and Intimacy,* is a testament to these groundbreaking stories. By raising their voices, these Muslim men are leading the way for other men to recognize that being open and honest about their feelings is not only okay—it's intimately connected to their lives and critical to their well-being.

It goes without saying—but we'll say it here anyway—that this book is not a theological treatise. It's a reflection of the real lives and experiences of Muslim men—fathers, brothers, sons, and partners.

We arranged these stories to mirror the ways in which our experiences about love, sex, and intimacy are shaped and evolve:

We begin with "Umma: It Takes a Village," in which our writers reflect—with humor and heartbreak—on the crucial role that family, friends, and community play in our sense of self and search for love.

The men in the second section, "Sirat: The Journey," share their stories about romantic, personal, and spiritual transformation. Their insights honestly—and bluntly—reveal how attitudes toward love, sex, and commitment can change over the course of our lives.

We end with "Sabr: In Sickness and in Health," in which our writers lift the facade of "happily ever after" to share what it really takes to keep a relationship going over a lifetime.

There's nothing like a good love story to connect us to one another and also help satisfy our curiosity about the lives of others—in this case, men. We welcome you to sit back—turn off your smartphones—and listen as these writers invite you to peek into their hearts, minds, and loves.

Umma: It Takes a Village

Soda Bottles and Zebra Skins

By Sam Pierstorff

Go ahead. Ask me if I am Muslim. It's true, I am. I'm white, Orange County, MTV-reality-show white. Beastie Boys circa 1986 white. The skater boy Avril Lavigne sang about white. Now, if you ask me how I came to be Muslim, I will need more time—enough time to tell you the long story about a Syrian girl from Aleppo who met a Kentucky redneck in the heart of Tennessee. Don't ask me how they got there.

Sure, he was a Korean War veteran, an English literature scholar, and a bit of an alcoholic, and she was Muslim, not entirely fluent in English, and wide-eyed with America's freedom—but the heart wants what the heart wants, right?

He was sympathetic to Islam, embracing the simplicity of one true God, instead of wrestling with the complexity of a trinity. And she was sympathetic to his vices—nothing a faithful wife couldn't cure, she thought. Of course, there were challenges—affairs, abuse, alcoholism—all of which were back-burnered when their two sons came along.

The firstborn was named by my mother—a Muslim name— Ahmed. He would become a treasure, a spiritual son, blessed the moment *al-Fatiha* was whispered into his ear at birth. The second born, out of fairness and compromise, was named by my father—an Anglo name, Samuel Johnson, after the eighteenth-century English critic and writer, whom he had studied. That's me. I would follow a more crooked path, spend more time outdoors than in, blessed at birth by my father's whiskey breath instead of his prayers.

✧ ✧ ✧

By fifth grade, the back burner could no longer contain the flames of my parents' marital problems. They split up. Our home went up in smoke. Poof. Gone. My father moved an hour westward toward the ocean, while my mother raised two boys alone in the desert of Riverside County, California, with all of the might left in her four-foot olive frame. She jarred my brother and me awake for dawn prayers and chauffeured us to the mosque on Fridays in her seat-beltless 1962 Studebaker while she tied her *hijab* in the rearview mirror and asked my brother to steer. Above all else, she taught us the five essential pillars of Islam: 1) believe in Allah and his final prophet, Muhammad; 2) pray five times a day; 3) don't look at girls; 4) don't speak to girls; 5) don't think about girls.

Girls, more than alcohol and pork, were *haram*. Hell was the tip of my mother's wooden spoon as she chased me after girls called the house, wanting to know why girls had my number. She yelled about religion and temptation and how kissing spread disease and French kissing made babies. God's anti-girlfriend stance was unfair and complicated. But my first crush was simple and powerful: Amy McKiernan. Every day I watched her on the playground, the sun in her blonde curls, her perfect pink-lipped smile. My heart was bursting every time Amy McKiernan pranced across the blacktop. My heart was not bursting with love for a deity that I could not see or touch or smell. Amy smelled like citrus, like rose petals, like love. One day after school, Amy and I circled behind the school's baseball dugout and nuzzled against each other. Her lips met mine. It was quick. Innocent. For a moment, I thought it would conjure the devil, but nothing happened. Just a spark that set fire to my heart. It felt like a tiny piece of heaven.

Though I could not see or touch or smell God, I could *feel* Him. The fear of Him, the weight of Him, the guilt of Him. My mother had taught me well. And that kept me from kissing Amy ever again, from holding her hand, or even talking to her after that first kiss.

In middle school, a bully named Hector called everyone a "jack-off."
I didn't know what he meant when he said, "Fuck you, Sammy, you
little jack-off." Then he made a fist and beat the air between his legs
with an invisible hammer. I had no idea what he was doing. I was
twelve, barely able to comb my hair without my brother helping me
mousse down the cowlicks in the back. My brother was always generous—trading shirts when mine fit like a potato sack, helping me
define cool words like "disembowel" and "castration." He knew it
all—a nose-in-a-book, glasses-wearing, king-of-all-nerds reader
with an IQ the size of Jupiter and a penchant for pleasing Mom. He
could read Arabic, too—slowly, right to left, one swooping letter at
a time. They sat together after prayer, hummed the thick vowels of
each *sura*. But not me. I was quick to launch myself outside as soon
as possible. There was a dumpster behind our apartment complex.
Inside were old, egg-stained *Playboys*, newspapers that advertised
strip clubs and phone-sex numbers with images of naked girls with
red stars on their nipples. That was my first exposure to pornography—long before the Internet. The torn pages of diaper-stained
magazines and newspaper ads were my porn sites; the dumpster
was my Google search engine. Pretty soon I figured out Hector's
little move. All the time, perhaps. I locked myself in the bathroom,
turned the faucet on high, and hammered until I thought I broke it.
But I didn't. This was puberty, coming too early.

In high school, my mom loosened up slightly. She didn't want to risk
losing us, and work kept her out of the house for ten hours a day, so
if she wanted to stay connected to us she had to become our friend
or we'd never speak again. Besides, we were nearly men, so what
choice did she have? We were growing facial hair, frosting our arm-
pits with deodorant, and sprouting muscles up and down our bodies. (Muslim workout tip: twenty push-ups after each *salat* = one

hundred push-ups per day.) My mother let my brother get away with his long, curly hair, and she let me get away with having a few girlfriends. There were more, of course, than she knew.

With these girls, I learned the fine art of dry humping, jean-on-jean friction so hard and fast I worried we might make a fire between our rubbing thighs. I knew intellectually that I was breaking countless rules of pious Muslim behavior by giving into lust. But it was like playing a game of chicken with God. How far could I walk toward the edge of the cliff without falling? I was young and horny enough to dip my toes past the edge, but strong enough to avoid falling from grace and permanently injuring myself. That was the game of balance I played. And I was winning. I never unbuckled or cut the ropes that tethered me to God. Loosened them a little, but never cut them completely.

The fear of sex that my mother introduced into our young minds stuck with me most of my life. Allah seemed pretty forgiving according to the *khutbahs* I heard, but in our house, sex was unforgivable—a one-way ticket to hell—and I didn't want to board that plane. Looking back, fear and guilt may have saved me from drowning in a world of high school sex and all the side effects that came with it. But there were still side effects, and that is where an American dad can help.

It had been months since we had last spoken, but I needed advice.

"Hey, Dad. It's Sam."

"Howdy, chief. How's your momma?"

"Fine."

"Brother?"

"Studying."

"How 'bout you?"

"My balls are killing me."

"What do you mean?"

"It feels like I got kicked in the nuts. Everything down there hurts. My stomach is sore too. I can hardly stand up."

"Sam, I am gonna ask you something, and you have to be honest with me. And don't worry, I won't tell your mother."

"Okay."

"Have you been getting a little hot and heavy with your girl-friend?"

"A little."

"Did you go all the way?"

"No!" I shouted.

"Well, then, there's your problem."

"What?"

"You're backed up. Ever shake a soda pop bottle with the cap on? It wants to burst. Don't it?"

"Yes."

"Right now, that soda bottle is your dick. It's gonna take a while to settle down. If it doesn't stop hurting in an hour, go rub it out."

I knew what he meant. He understood male plumbing. I had a genital clog and two options: be patient or beat off. I should have prayed—dropped two *rakat* to ask Allah for forgiveness and *sabr.* Minutes later, I relieved myself and took a long nap afterward. I later read that I had experienced "blue balls"—epididymal hypertension or vasocongestion. Unlike unicorns and leprechauns, blue balls are very real and very painful.

In college, among my Muslim male friends, which, *alhamdulillah,* I had plenty of at Long Beach State University, no one talked about masturbation or virginity. We all just assumed they both existed in our lives. The running joke was that every Muslim male was Hanafi until he got married because the Hanafi school made masturbation permissible, but only to prevent *zina* or to release sexual tension (not just desire). Otherwise, it was forbidden. I never asked, but I am pretty sure my male Muslim friends released a lot of sexual "ten-sion" in college. I read somewhere that 99 percent of men do it, and the other 1 percent lie about it. We were the 1 percent. Muslim men, growing up in the United States of pornography and booty shorts, are not immune. Guilt ridden? Yes. Overflowing with regret and shame? Perhaps. Full of prayers for greater strength in the face of temptation? Every *Jumma*. But definitely not immune.

Marriage, I used to say, was the cure. Actually, I may have sub-consciously been paraphrasing the Prophet, who said to young people, "Whoever among you can support a wife should marry, for that is more modest for the gaze and safer for your private parts." Marriage is a life raft wherein one's libido can float along safely as it sails down a choppy river of American hypersexuality.

"Think about it, *amigos*," I would say to my college buddies. "What great sin do we commit that won't be cured by marriage? We're actually pretty good Muslims when you think about it. We don't drink or snort cocaine. We don't kill people or steal cars. We don't blow shit up, contrary to the stereotype. We help old ladies across the street. We donate food to homeless shelters and send money overseas to Palestine and Afghanistan to help build schools."

"Yeah," Rashid interjected, "I helped a neighbor move her couch up two flights of stairs yesterday."

"Remember when that guy's Buick broke down on Pine Avenue and we pushed him out of the street so he wouldn't get hit?" Mo-hammed added.

We reminisced. There was no shortage of good deeds among us. We were diligent about Friday prayers, and fasting, and *salat* five times a day (or at least four—*fajr* was tough).

"With this one tiny exception of lust and our obsession with girls, we're pretty good guys, right?" I pronounced.

"Dude, you're droppin' knowledge, *mashAllah*."

Everyone started puffing up with a sense of confidence that quietly slipped away every time an overly bearded fellow or scowling auntie at the mosque insinuated with their eyes that we were girl-crazy.

"Now we just need to find ourselves some wives."

Graduate school was on the horizon. I chose to stay at Long Beach State University to complete a master's degree in English because they offered me a class to teach. I was older, more mature. My libido was tamer than it had been, and my heart was open to real love, the kind that is sustainable and permanent. At *Jumma* prayers, I found myself drifting, my eyes falling upon little boys in *thobes* dragging toy cars across the prayer carpets, or infants asleep in their fathers' arms as the fathers continued to pray, careful not to wake the baby. I wanted a family. The next stage of life was calling out to me. I could sense the seismic shift in my brain, moving from lust to wanting lifelong love.

By my second year of grad school, I was working full-time at the university, teaching composition courses and coordinating educational programs for inner-city youth. I made a decent wage for a twenty-four-year-old kid and owned a new black Toyota pickup. What girl wouldn't want to marry me? My quest began.

There were rumblings within my inner circle of mostly Indian American Muslim friends about a girl named Ruhi. She was Indian American, too. Some said we should meet. We'd be perfect for each other, they said.

"Why?" I asked.

"Because she's short like you!"

"Is that the only reason?"

"She's also cute. She's funny. She likes to read."

"Read what?"

"Books, stupid."

No one mentioned faith, hers or mine. The irony of Muslim dating is that very few people mention Islam. That's the easy part: believe, pray, fast, donate, hajj. If you're both Muslim, it's really a matter of attraction and compatibility—and a short, cute, funny reader of books sounded divine.

I'd never dated Indian American girls, but in college I was a cowboy surrounded by Indians. My best male friends were Indian American; their girlfriends were too. At the mosques in Southern California, there were more *dupattas* than hijabs, more *biryani* served at *iftar* dinner than kibbeh. The comfort of my Arab/white palette (e.g., meatloaf and hummus) was left in the wake as I dined on tandoori chicken and naan. My tastes changed. Drastically. I began to marvel at the thick, black, glimmering hair of Indian girls, their big eyes glazed with green eye shadow, gold bangles clinking up and down their forearms. All the white girls I'd ever crushed on became pale ghosts rising from my memory and disappearing into an exotic, marigold sky.

And then I saw her on campus by a dandelion-shaped fountain. She was with some girls I knew. But Ruhi was different. Blue eye shadow, blue jeans, flip-flops. A little shorter than the rest and way more casual—a blend between a laid-back surfer and Aishwarya Rai.

"Hey, Sam," a girl with a gold nose ring shouted. "This is my friend, Ruhi."

Ruhi looked up. Our eyes met. I first noticed the perfect heart-shaped dip in the center of her upper lip, right below her nose, or was it her eyes? Honey-colored, almond-shaped. She smiled. I read deeply into that smile. While some have seen their whole lives flash before their eyes, I could see *her* life flashing before *my* eyes. I saw kindness and generosity. I saw adversity and strength. I saw a pair of lips prone to giggling, and I knew I could make her laugh. I saw, above all else, familiarity. If a face could be described as nonjudgmental, this was it—beautiful and bright with love and acceptance. I wanted her all to myself.

I finally found my voice.

"Oh, you're Ruhi?"

Her: "Yeah?"

Me: "We need to talk."

Her: "We do?"

Me: "Yes, we definitely do."

I didn't know what I needed to talk to her about, but I knew immediately that I needed to spend time with her. She was the one. It was that simple. Attractive. Muslim. A little shorter than I was, which was rare. Perfect. Now all I needed was to talk to her to work out the details of our wedding. I was in a hurry. My "private parts" would not be safe for very much longer.

Courting Ruhi was not unlike most young Muslim courtships in America. You tell your mother that you're going to school to study, and then you meet your boyfriend or girlfriend at a coffee shop or at the movies or at a bookstore. On our first date, we tried to keep it halal. We knew the Prophet had said, "Whenever a man is alone with a woman, the devil makes a third," so we brought along a skinny business major named Rashid. He was technically not a *wali*, but he was *like* a brother to us both, so that had to count for something.

We went to BJ's restaurant in downtown Long Beach and ate deep-dish pizza. Rashid and I sat on one side of the booth while Ruhi sat in the center of the other. She was dressed modestly in a purple sweater, thin and V-necked, with a white top underneath— silver hoops swinging from her earlobes. Her eye shadow was dusted with specks of silver glitter, or maybe I'm remembering incorrectly. Maybe *she* was sparkling.

The steaming pan of pizza rested atop our table. Everyone stared at the last thick slice, but no one wanted to appear greedy. Eventually Rashid, with his blessed metabolism, ate it, and through greasy bites—cheese dangling from his lips—broke the awkward silence that had settled over our table.

"So are you guys gonna get married or what?"

In the minds of most Muslims, it is that easy. Find a Muslim girl. Get married. Simple. No personality tests, common tastes in music, complicated feelings, long talks about future goals. "Love" is a manufactured emotion designed by the West to fall in and out of rather than a simple choice. Do it or don't. Period.

"Your kid's skin will look like coffee with too much cream," Rashid teased. In his mind, the wedding was over and we had become parents before the Pizookie had been served for dessert.

Rashid became a fixture in our dating lives, the tagalong kid we couldn't get rid of. For weeks we dated (all three of us) and saw one another on campus, but Ruhi and I needed to be alone. We had heard of a place called *The Next Level*, and we both decided it was time to take our relationship there without an audience.

Less than a month after Ruhi and I met, her parents left for Tanzania, where they were born and raised. They would be there for three weeks. At nineteen, Ruhi was old enough to be left behind to finish her semester of college without disruption, despite her mother pleading otherwise: "A Muslim girl should not be alone in the house. It is not safe."

Her father reminded her mother that Ruhi was a big girl. There was money in an envelope, gas in the car, relatives nearby. She would be fine. After all, this was not the African savannah. No lion was lurking in the shadows, ready to pounce.

I was no predator, but this was a chance I wasn't willing to pass up. It was 7:45 p.m., Saturday night, when I began my drive down the 405 freeway to Redondo Beach for my first Rashid-less date with the girl I was beginning to love. Until now, our only time alone had been phone conversations lasting deep into the night. We traded books and poems, shared stories about growing up. Neither of us had had it easy, but we both had each other to look forward to now. My stomach boomed with anxiety. I played Metallica loudly in the car and yelled along with James Hetfield the whole way there.

My index finger shook above the doorbell to her house. Then she emerged, framed in the doorway, backlit by lamps with severed gazelle hooves for bases. She invited me inside. I was in a different world. On the shelves, Qur'ans everywhere, a tapestry of Mecca near the door, a million white dots swirling around the Kaaba.

On the opposite wall, a zebra skin splayed out like it had just been skinned. One false move, I thought, and that might be my skin up there if her dad ever caught me in his house . . . with his daughter . . . alone.

"Want some chai?" Ruhi asked.

She'd already made some, a pot of black tea and milk brewed thick with cardamom and cloves. She added sugar and served it to me with a cookie on the side—a spongy orange golf ball that she called *laddu.*

I stirred my chai, blowing into the cup to cool it down.

"Do you think our kids will have skin this color?" I asked.

She didn't look pleased. Too soon, I thought, too soon. Suddenly, there was a knock at the front door. I leapt off my stool, her eyes wide as dinner plates. And then a louder knock. With a family of a thousand cousins and a hundred aunts, many of whom lived in the area, the chances were pretty good that a relative was at the door.

"Hide in my room! Hurry!" Ruhi yanked me into her bedroom, pushed me into the closet, then pulled me out just as fast.

"Outside! Go out the French doors. Hide in the backyard!"

I hurdled over her bed, burst through the double doors into her backyard, and pinned myself against a tree and the stucco wall behind her house. I was shaking. My belly was full of bullet holes and scalding hot chai was leaking out. I wasn't afraid of God. I was afraid of whoever was at the door.

"Hey girl, what are you all dressed up for? Going out?"

It was her cousin, an NBA-tall, slightly gangster-looking guy named, I would later learn, Maqbul. He was sent by an auntie. "Trust-worthy" is not a word often associated with a young, single, beautiful, Muslim girl in the U.S. At least not in Urdu. So a family henchman had been sent over to check on Ruhi.

"I'm not going anywhere. I'm staying home."

Through the gap in the drapes, I could see Ruhi and the lanky shadow of Maqbul. It was clear that she was trying to keep him at the front door, out of view of our two cups of half-drunk chai in the kitchen like spilled blood at a crime scene. She had one hand pressed against his chest, her triceps flexing as she pushed him away.

"Get out of here, Maq. I need to take a shower and go to bed."

Good excuse, I thought. He persisted, but Ruhi was strong. He never crossed the threshold. She closed the door behind him, locked it, and came to fetch me from the yard.

"He's gone. You can come in."

"I think I better get going. That was too close," I said, still shaking like an old man with Parkinson's.

That was the end of our first and only date. We were too scared to go out in public. We'd be seen. We'd be caught. We'd be judged. I had to do this the right way or not at all.

Two months went by. Two months of long letters, coffee on campus, and poetry readings. Ruhi's friends would drag her to my events to hear me read poems, and she would stand in the back blushing when a line about love was clearly aimed at her. She was my muse, and I wanted to hold on to her forever.

It was Sunday, blissfully warm near her home in Redondo Beach. That's where I met her parents in person. I brought my mother and brother along. We sat in the parlor beneath the splayed zebra skin. It was awkward to be there again—even though I was invited this time.

I proposed. Officially. Halal style. I told her parents how much I loved their daughter, how I would care for her better than I cared for myself, how nothing in this world meant more to me than she did. Everyone was in tears. Mostly me and Ruhi, though. We were softies. We had found each other in a peculiar world, and we had nothing left to hide.

Six months later, we married and moved from Southern California to Modesto, where I landed a full-time, tenure-track teaching position at Modesto Junior College. Once there, we began to create our own world where, for the past twelve years, we have lived and laughed and cried a whole lot more—like when our first son was born and had to spend a week in the NICU; or when our daughter was born after Ruhi had so desperately wanted a girl; or when our littlest came out, fired up and pumping his tiny fists. All with skin like coffee with too much cream. All beautiful, *alhamdulillah.*

Looking back, I regret never having that first "real" date. So some nights, Ruhi and I turn our suburban kitchen into a dance floor. Instead of a strobe light, our oldest son stands on a chair and flicks the light switch on and off. Our daughter picks songs on an iPad as our little guy hops around like a bunny rabbit. But at least admission is free, and our club never closes, and our song never stops playing.

Mother's Curse

By Arsalan Ahmed

My mother was strangely calm as I announced my intention to marry Anne.

It should not have come as a surprise. She had met Anne several times since we'd graduated from university in Massachusetts three years ago. On my most recent visit to see my family in Karachi, Anne had sent a hand-knitted scarf for her. "You do realize it's never cold enough there for a scarf?" I said affectionately, only to be shushed.

It was a Saturday, in the summer of 2002. We were having a garage sale at our Boston condo before moving to Geneva, where Anne was to start a new job working on refugee issues at the United Nations. I was on the phone with my mother as Anne battled the early birds.

"I can't talk right now," Ammi said. "Here is your father."

"No, sir, the Jetta is not for sale," I heard through the window.

Although Abu appeared to have surmised what was going on, he listened politely as I repeated my speech. "Are you sure?" he asked. I could hear Ammi wailing in the background.

"Yes," I said, but he was gone. Ammi was back on the phone.

"Do whatever you want," she shrieked. "But know one thing: you will never be happy."

"What?" I asked, confused.

"You will never be happy. Never. Not after giving someone so much pain."

She hung up.

Later, outside the garage, a family of ducks pecked at our feet. I gave a young Pakistani couple a tape recording of Zia Mohyeddin reading classic works of Urdu literature. They were thrilled. After they left, I cried a little. The ducks squawked while Anne patted my back.

That night, Ammi tried, determinedly but inexpertly, to kill herself.

Two days later, I was on a flight to Karachi. The drive from the airport was grim, the mood at my parents' house funereal. Indeed, I have been to more cheerful funerals. From Ammi's chilling silences to her searing rage, I numbly plodded through what were, until that point, the most difficult days of my life.

Quite quickly, I discovered the three deficiencies that doomed Anne.

Religion. How will a Christian adapt to a pious Muslim household?

Anne had lost faith years ago, around the same time that the sons of the pious Muslim household last saw the inside of a mosque.

Race. How will a blonde and freckled girl live in this racially pure city, purer since 9/11, when the last tourists left in a hurry?

I had grown up in Karachi. But Anne and I had no plans to live there, although this was a point best left for future discussion.

Culture. How will a child of divorced parents from a morally bankrupt society fit into a traditional, extended family? What will people say?

Years later, when Ammi had two divorced sons and a Pakistani daughter-in-law from hell, I would be better equipped to respond. Then, I merely blinked.

My brother, Bhayeea, was nonchalant. "Come, bull, kill me," he said bemusedly. "You couldn't just have continued quietly living with her?"

He had a point. Anne and I had been living together for almost three years. If Ammi knew, she never said so. On Anne's last birthday, when I proposed with a sapphire ring, we had been giddily happy. I had only worked up the courage to give Ammi the news a week later.

Now it was done. Lines had been drawn, intercontinental curses cast, pills swallowed, scarves knitted. I waded through the aftermath the best I could.

A week later I flew back to Boston, marital discussions placed in a deep freezer, in my father's words, until Ammi was well enough to resume battle.

"Her condition is such that any adverse action on your part could have dire consequences," Abu warned.

"Dire," he repeated, furrowing his brow meaningfully. I nodded, as if I understood.

She only became well enough two years later. Two years of an uneasy peace. Minor but punishing skirmishes aside, there were hardly any engagements to speak of. I am intrinsically nonconfrontational—cowardly, Anne said in exasperation—so I handled the conflict the only way I knew how: by avoiding it. Grimly, Ammi and I waged a cold war. Politeness was our weapon, Abu and Bhayeea our proxies. She had the strategic advantage of emotional blackmail, of course, but I had the self-righteousness of youth. That and Dylan. *Your sons and your daughters/Are beyond your command*, I would hum often, tunelessly but with great earnestness.

Stubbornly, I refused to marry without Ammi's consent, however grudging. Our conflict was one of ideas, not actions. Victory was not simply getting what one wanted, but doing so with the adversary's blessing. She reciprocated, shunning the soap-operatic Pakistani mother's classic move of disowning a son, never again speaking his name. Which was what an uncle of hers had done some forty years prior, when an errant son married a Canadian woman. "He never saw his son's face again, not even from his deathbed," Ammi said, darkly and not very subtly.

My resolve and Anne's patience lasted two years. Eventually, I announced that we were looking at venues in Boston, debating food options and guest lists. All of a sudden, the iron curtain lifted, amid much surprise and rejoicing. There was a surge of last-minute, but ultimately halfhearted, resistance. "So it has come to this," Ammi sniffed. But the passion of the past was gone, as if Gorbachev had secretly embraced capitalist decadence in his home, but had to keep up appearances at the politburo.

The bigger surprise came when Ammi proclaimed, to universal disbelief, that if a wedding were to take place, it had to be done properly: in Karachi, with many guests, a *dholki*, a *gharara*, a *nikah*, and a *maulvi* sahib. (We later negotiated the *maulvi* sahib down to an uncle.) "You can't stop a speaker's tongue," she said on the phone as I scratched my head. "So why try? We will do your wedding with great fanfare."

A month later, on the night of the *dholki*, sipping chilled Bubble Up on my parents' lawn under a puzzled April moon, I wondered what the fuss had been all about. Was it all an elaborate act, at best a grudging acceptance of what Ammi could not control? People never change, I had always believed. Or do they? She certainly appeared to have embraced Anne like the daughter she'd never had but had always wanted. She told her how lucky I was to have found her, taught her how to make *masoor ki daal*, gently corrected her for using her left hand while saying *adaab* to an elderly great-aunt, took her bangle shopping, and showered her with gifts and affection.

"I never spoke ill of her," Ammi explained later, hazily and not entirely truthfully, clarifying her position on her former nemesis, the child of a broken home from a morally bankrupt society. "I opposed the idea of her, the foreign girl who wouldn't understand our family and would break us apart." By then Ammi was busy battling a new bane, my brother's first, Pakistani wife, and her thoughts on cultural compatibility and the clash of civilizations had evolved considerably.

I don't think it was pretense, either. Months later, when Ammi came to visit us in Switzerland, she seemed genuinely happy, perhaps the happiest I have ever seen her. Walking by the lake in Montreux, up to the Chateau de Chillon, she held Anne's hand, casually, as mothers and daughters do in my clichéd imagination. For our first wedding anniversary, she gave Anne a sari, and took us to the roof-top restaurant at the Pearl Continental, in Karachi. There was cake and laughter. Later, when Anne wanted to ride a camel on Sea View beach, it was Ammi who negotiated the price with the camel wallah. "This is my daughter, not some memsahib," she declared, as he sputtered helplessly about his small, small children. I should have been concerned, but I was merely content.

Retracting a curse is a hard business, harder perhaps than breaking it.

A year later, when Anne spiraled inexorably into psychological despair, I thought about the curse a great deal. Curses, hexes, the evil eye. I clutched at anything that could explain my crumbling life. Nothing did. "It's not you, it's something I'm going through," Anne said, between sobs, during what I told myself was a rare moment of sanity.

One day she was gone, leaving behind a note and bookshelves with empty, sullen spaces. In the white kitchen trashcan, I carefully burned the note and watched the blaze until it died out. The following week, I packed up the remainders, and moved back to Boston.

When I had picked up enough of life's pieces, I called Ammi to tell her that Anne was not finishing up a project in Switzerland and would not, as far as I knew, move to Boston to be with me.

Ammi listened quietly.

"You'll never find a girl like her again," she said, not triumphantly, but with sorrow, without malice. "Never."

The Ride

By Ramy Eletreby

Corey's favorite saying: "Buy the ticket, take the ride."

I suppose I should have seen a red flag when he quoted eccentric countercultural figures like Hunter S. Thompson. There was a pulsing rhythm and fearlessness to how he experienced life that was more fast-paced, more spirited, than I was used to.

I was twenty-two years old in 2003, wrapped tightly as a spool of twine. I walked a very straight line. My adventurous side was limited to speeding on the freeway, usually for a few seconds at a time, because I was certain California Highway Patrol was waiting for me one hundred yards ahead. Nor did I carry a surfboard in the back of my truck, unlike almost every other boy in south Orange County. I did not plan my schedule around the tides, because the waves were always too unpredictable, too uncontrollable for me. The ocean view from my parents' house was enough. I did not need to touch the sand to know the beach was there.

Look, but don't touch. Self-restraint was what I carried.

I had come out to myself when I was fifteen. Some friends and I had gone to see a new play in downtown LA about homophobia and machismo in Mexican American boxing circles during the 1950s. When a handsome and muscular Latino actor stripped down to nothing and took a shower for five full minutes on stage, I felt all the blood rush to my face. It rushed below my waist, too. My eyes gazed downward, embarrassed to be looking at something so raw and so enticing. I had never seen anything more beautiful, and I knew that I would never be able to look at a man the same way again. Driving home after the performance, I was buzzing. I couldn't keep to myself what had happened, what seeing that naked man did to me. When I told my friends, they told me that I was probably gay. I immediately burst into tears.

I was a master at suppression. My father was chairman of the local Islamic center and my mother was principal of the Sunday school. My family was a pillar of the community. Everyone knew my parents and, by extension, their children. My parents were good at keeping my sister, my brother, and me on a short leash. They insisted that we apply to colleges in Southern California so we could live at home under their watchful eyes. They didn't want us to fall prey to the temptations of college. I didn't pay for my college education, so I attended UC Irvine, my parents' choice, a twenty-minute ride up Pacific Coast Highway. I never went to parties. I never stayed out past ten o'clock at night, unless I was in rehearsals for a play.

I knew I was privileged. I was the only one of my college circle who had a thirty-five-thousand-dollar salary within weeks of graduation. That was just one of the many perks of my father owning a business. Allah was so generous with me that faith and gratitude were the only things I could give back. I prayed to Allah five times a day and read chapters of the Qur'an almost every night.

I spent years shaming myself and "praying the gay away." With some tenacity, I was successful at ignoring my desires and diverting that energy into being a better Muslim. Those moments of restriction then became signals to give more praise to Allah. When Allah couldn't feed the flame, the suppression manifested in compulsive eating and shopping. I was a storm of paisley and chocolate.

Staring at boys at the gym was my treat. I convinced myself that Allah had provided me with eye candy so I could satisfy my urges without crossing any lines. The furtive glances I stole at those surfer boys—white, hairless, perfect—changing in the locker room was Allah granting me pleasure. In secret, of course. I never spoke to anyone. I felt like a creeper. And I was.

When Corey came up to me in the locker room, I thought he was going to confront me. I was sure that he must have seen me staring at him in the mirror. Now he was going to humiliate me and ensure that I never stared at anyone again. Instead, he smiled and invited me to join him in the Jacuzzi and chat because I was "not like the other guys here." I wasn't sure what he meant and didn't know if I should be offended. His pale blue eyes were too gentle for me to be critical of anything he said.

I certainly wasn't like the other guys there. I was brown, hairy, and chubby. I was twice the size of any of the other boys. Was it my Arabness, my otherness, that intrigued Corey? Was he fetishizing me, as many did after 9/11? Or was it my height, my extra largeness, that caught Corey's attention? Was he one of those twinks with a Daddy complex? What exactly did he want of me? It would be crazy to think he was interested in anything physical. Gay boys my age, especially the white ones, never showed me any attention.

I don't remember what Corey and I discussed in the Jacuzzi that first night. All I remember thinking was that this was probably the first boy my own age who'd ever approached me and had a genuine curiosity about me. This beautiful guy was interested in what I had to say. He probably never realized how special he made me feel in that moment. He had no idea that he was the first person who made me feel seen. I remember rushing home afterward to pray to Allah, to express gratitude for bringing Corey into my life. I think I started loving him instantly, from the moment we lowered ourselves into that hot tub. I fell quickly and I fell hard. I was so overcome with *feeling* that I started unraveling. There are few things as fragile as an untouched heart.

The beginnings of our friendship played out like a John Hughes film: calling each other late at night, writing each other "notes" (texts), hanging out in each other's bedrooms, meeting each other's families, driving up and down the coast, finding quiet spots where we'd smoke weed and get high. Every moment we shared together had an underlying current of angst and sexual tension.

Early on, he made it clear that he just wanted to be friends. I didn't want to admit that the feelings between us flowed in only one direction. He must've known that I was secretly infatuated with every particle of his being. The way his hair caught the light, the way his eyes changed color based on the shirt he was wearing, the tattoo on his arm of the Cancer astrological sign.

There's an interesting shift that can happen when you start loving someone. Suddenly, you forget yourself and take on the interests of the other person. Corey liked to drink, pop pills, and shoot guns.

"That's what white people do best," he would say.

He was shocked when I told him I'd never been drunk before. During our first summer together, he took care of that. He invited me over to play poker with his dad, and for every hand dealt, he would pour tequila. His dad chuckled seeing me squirm at every sip. It wasn't until later, when I was lying facedown on Corey's bed in a pool of my own vomit, that they stopped to think that maybe I needed some monitoring.

Corey had a locked black box under his bed, which held a sleek, all-black, lightweight Glock pistol. I was all nerves when he showed it to me for the first time. I had never held a gun before, nor had I wanted to. The idea of having something so destructive in my hands was terrifying. When Corey placed it into my shaking hands, I held it like it was the most fragile piece of glass. He assured me that it wasn't loaded, showing me every nook and cranny, taking it apart and putting it back together again, with great pride. The gleam in his eyes was frightening, but also incredibly sexy.

He took me to a shooting range hidden under the freeway, a place near my home that I'd never known existed. He stood behind me, body pressed against mine, demonstrating how to hold the gun. His arms were lightly wrapped around mine. His hands enclosed my hands holding the gun. His finger rested on my finger, pulling the trigger as we fired my first shot together. I never felt closer to him. Something about guns made him feel like more of a man. He had three straight older brothers and major issues with masculinity. Almost everything he did was an assertion of his manhood. I wanted him to know that he was all the man I ever needed.

We played Led Zeppelin and sang with Bob Dylan. We danced with Walt Whitman, and we partied with Hunter S. Thompson. We spoke of God and his prophets Muhammad and Jesus and Gautama Buddha. Every being worth exalting, we did. With every breath we exhaled together, I fell deeper and deeper. Our minds were connected, and I'm certain that our souls were too. But not our bodies. That was just my secret fantasy.

I never explicitly told him how I felt. Corey would often speak about boys in the gym he found attractive. He usually went for twinks like himself, but a few years younger, around eighteen. To me, they were little boys who hadn't finished growing. He never looked at me the way he looked at them. He had to know how I felt, but he still wanted to be my friend. I thought I could be happy with that. A platonic friendship was better than not having him in my life at all.

A year after meeting Corey, I had finally moved out of my parents' house in Orange County and up to LA with some of my best friends from college. My friendship with Corey had made me realize I needed to distance myself physically from my family, to uncover parts of my identity that I'd ignored.

I was out and open with my friends in LA, but donned a mask around family. I'd become an expert at compartmentalizing, separating my identity into distinct parts that never interacted. Like many young gay men dealing with internalized shame, I initially became caught up in a perpetual cycle of partying and first dates. Sometimes, if the sex was good, there would be a second date, and, on extremely rare occasions, a third.

I saw Corey regularly whenever I drove down to OC to see my family. Shortly after I moved, he had a new boyfriend, seventeen-year-old Dave. It always irked me that despite the strong mental connection Corey and I had, despite our long talks about the complexities of religion and politics, he fell for immature teens who did not know much beyond Beyoncé and Britney Spears. His penchant for young femme boys was another way of asserting his masculinity.

I was a witness to Corey's pill popping. He always carried Valium, and took up to six tablets a day. He said his doctor prescribed them for anxiety, but that was a half-truth. He'd pop three pills with his first cocktail. I never took more than one. He would drive down to Tijuana and buy a hundred tablets in some random pharmacy that he knew well. He once took me with him. I felt uncomfortable scoring illegal pharmaceutical drugs in Mexico. I didn't understand it. Why couldn't we smoke weed like we normally did? Marijuana made me feel stimulated and connected. Valium made me groggy and detached.

Corey convinced me to go to Burning Man in 2004. He said he had to see the epicenter of counterculture. I read about the annual weeklong arts festival in the middle of the desert, where people build a temporary community together. Normally, that would be the last place on Earth I'd want to be. But I would have gone to the tundra for him.

On the way to "the Burn" we stopped in San Francisco. Corey wanted to go to the famed City Lights bookstore. City Lights had published many of his favorite Beat works, including Allen Ginsberg's epic poem "Howl," which we recited countless times while drunk and stoned in his bedroom. I had a surprise for him. I looked up the address of the apartment where Ginsberg was living when he wrote the poem. It was only a few blocks from the bookstore. As we stood outside apartment H, Corey held his palm against the cold gray door and looked down. I heard him sniffling and saw him wipe his eyes. My heart melted—or exploded. I can't remember which. All I wanted to do was grab him, hold him tight, and tell him that if he let me, I would always be there to do special things like that for him.

I came out to my family after Burning Man. The months following were the worst time of my life. It started when I was cast in a play as a character named Hatam, a young, gay, Muslim, Arab American man who was out to his friends but closeted to his family. Just like me.

The local Muslim community, *my* community, heard about the gay character and boycotted the production. After that, the *Los Angeles Times* called me for an interview. When the interviewer asked me how I reconciled doing the play as a Muslim, I responded, "Because I am gay and I am Muslim. I can't just be *part* of myself." That was my coming out. What should have been private became very public.

The morning the article was printed, the news spread across Southern California like one of its raging wildfires. By ten o'clock, the story had been forwarded to my father via e-mail. The national LGBTQ newsmagazine the *Advocate* called me a day later for another interview. Overnight, I became the poster boy for gay Muslims in the U.S. I felt exposed in the spotlight. The media blitz didn't last too long, but it reached enough people in my community to humiliate my parents.

> *"How could you do this to us?"*
> *"Everyone is talking about us and saying shameful things about our son."*
> *"You're on a slippery slope and you need to get professional help immediately."*
> *"Go run to your disgusting friends, who taught you that it was okay to be so filthy."*

I wanted to shut myself off from the world. I wasn't interested in seeing anyone, especially Corey. I did not expect him to understand how I felt. He came out when he was sixteen, and his parents barely flinched. He brought boyfriends home to meet his family. He had no idea what it was like to have parents tell him he was filthy and disgusting. He had no idea what it was like to have to defend his sanity, or to have his older siblings ask inappropriate questions about his sex life.

One night Corey called while I was having a fight with my brother and sister. It was one o'clock in the morning when he picked me up. He took me down to the beach, and I broke down and cried. I remember telling him how much I hated my family and Allah. I said I was through with Islam. That I could no longer be part of a faith that teaches people to turn on their own flesh and blood. Though he was agnostic, he consoled me. He said that the future was full of possibilities and that one day I might find my way back to Allah. He knew how much I enjoyed being a Muslim and didn't want me to lose that part of myself.

That was the first and last time he ever held me. I don't know how long we sat together on the beach. It could've been just twenty minutes. It felt like I was in his arms all night.

Four months later, Dave called me. He told me that Corey hadn't woken up that morning. He had taken a lot of pills the night before and his heart had stopped. I can't remember the rest of the conversation. It sounded like a joke. Corey was always taking something, and he always bounced back. Why should this time be any different?

It was a punch in the gut. I started kicking and screaming and demanding that Allah apologize for doing something so unimaginable. There was no way Allah would allow me to lose both the love and respect of my family and the only man I ever loved just months apart. He could not be that cruel. All I could think of was that moment Corey had held me on the beach. Why hadn't I told him that I loved him? Would that have changed anything?

I remember looking at the Zen Wisdom calendar sitting on my bathroom sink, still in disbelief about what I'd been told. That day's saying was "Sometimes we lose people at a very young age. They are angels on Earth reminding us of impermanence." Chuckling, fighting back tears, the only thing I remember saying was "He bought one ticket too many, and took his final ride."

A reminder of impermanence is important. But I wish the reminder didn't have to hurt so much.

It took me a long time to trust Allah after that. To forgive Him for turning my parents and my community against me, for taking Corey, and for turning His back on me. Over the next few years, I stopped fasting during Ramadan and started playing with various states of lucidity. I used marijuana and alcohol mostly, but sometimes harder substances. The ups and downs of a fragile emotional state, with no spiritual anchor, took its toll, and self-medication sometimes felt necessary.

It wasn't until almost a decade later that I reestablished a spiritual relationship with Allah. It happened one night at the theatre in New York City when I went to see a play called *Coming Out Muslim: Radical Acts of Love*, written and performed by Wazina Zondon and Terna Tilley-Gyado. These two Muslim women celebrated being Muslim and homosexual. Their poetic language echoed the poetry of the Qur'an, as if the play had come down from Allah as another revelation. It was the first time I saw a *whole* gay Muslim person, living happily, balancing both identities, and the multitudes in between, without conflict. My tears flowed and wouldn't stop.

In the words of one character: "Allah makes Muslims. Allah makes queers. I've never felt Islam asks me to be something other than what I am. If Allah is closer than my own jugular vein—*Ya Khalaq! Ya Bari! Ya Mussawir!*—the source of its blood and beat, how could I despise myself?"

As an applied theater artist and practitioner, I know all about the blurring of the lines between drama and reality, and the power theater possesses to advocate and to liberate. Once again, the theater pushed me to reconceive myself. If my relationship with Allah had been so fraught for years, was there anyone to blame other than myself? Wasn't it my own anger and my own hurt that kept me away?

Nothing lasts forever, and every being will die. I'm grateful to possess that wisdom now. I wish that, at twenty-four, I'd had the maturity to know how to guard my heart better. I wish I could go back and tell myself to hold onto a piece of it rather than give it all away, especially to someone who couldn't keep it safe. Today, ten years later, I still carry Corey with me, in whatever is left of my heart. Sometimes it feels like my heart was swallowed with his last batch of pills. Though it was once filled with love, it now sits empty.

But I recognize that I am the only one who stands in the way of my own happiness. I am the only one who can fill my heart with love again. If I learn to love myself more, I will rediscover my capacity to love others.

I need to practice more self-care, to learn healing and forgiveness. I need to recite Allah's ninety-nine names more. *Ya Khalaq* (the Creator), *Ya Bari* (the Maker from Nothing), *Ya Mussawir* (the Bestower of Forms). When I forget Allah, I forget myself.

Today, I remind myself to count my blessings, to recognize that my parents are still a part of my life, even if they will never see me the way I want them to. I try to practice gratitude, to remember Corey as the gift from Allah that I originally saw him to be. I continue to ask for forgiveness, to cleanse myself of the hurt and anger I have caused others, especially my family.

There is no joy without sorrow. Life is full of oppositions. We are all large and we contain multitudes. My challenge is to run to Allah when I feel like running away.

A Grown-Ass Man

By Alykhan Boolani

Terrified Immigrant Syndrome

I gave up trying to meet women at *jamat khana* years ago. These days, I'm mostly in it for the aunties, the uncles, and Bapa's chai.

I haven't given up on religion itself per se, but I've got my devotional disregard down to a science: Friday night *dua* starts at eight and is over by half past. At five till, I glance at my wrist, making note of the day and time. At ten past, I attempt to fix my hair in the mirror by my front door. North Oakland is a solid fifteen to Alameda, on the 24. By the time I slide into the corporate-office-park-unit-cum-*masjid*—demarcated only by a yellowed inkjet printout of an American flag with the words UNITED WE STAND in Times New Roman—prayers are damn-near over and the first eyes on me are always Pops's. He sits in the chairs by the door, outside the prayer hall, with all the other *budha bhais*, whose knees and backs keep them off the ground where the rest of us sit. He looks me up and down, looks at the clock, looks right back at me, and grins to himself while shaking his head. I choose to interpret this as playful disappointment.

Fortunately my mother sits inside, usually up front. I'm glad to know that she doesn't have to witness my weekly ritual of cultivated neglect. We are, however, keenly aware of each other; and in the sad state of affairs, weekly neglect is far better than downright absence. Like a hostage situation, my attendance holds Ma's last hope for my life on *sirat al-Mustaqim* by its throat. Otherwise, I could become like so-and-so Auntie's kids who stopped coming altogether, and then became alcohol-and-drug addicts, and then married—*gasp*—the whites!

Unrestricted hyperbole is a well-documented effect of Terrified Immigrant Syndrome (TIS). Thus my mother links a bit of religious laxity to wholesale cultural downfall—another friend's mother has been known to link Jolt Cola to eventual cocaine use. But admittedly, her fears are, if dramatic, not unfounded. Her central cultural wish of keeping *Shia Imami Isma'ilism* conjugal, in my sordid generation, is quickly becoming, outside of the motherland, a dream deferred.

I mean the story of Ma and Pops? It may as well be another dimension of space/time: the two grew up in flats opposite each other, on a street bookended by a grand *Isma'ili jamat khana* and an *Isma'ili* grammar school, in a part of Karachi where the cultural, economic, and social life was *Isma'ili*. It was not an arranged match, though a degree of city planning may have been involved.

The Mantra

The table, crowded by hot and slick plates, looks to be alive. The overhead fan cuts the fluorescents into a flicker, and the feast's glistening seems to dance in the light. We've been eating like this every night since we arrived in Karachi, around a long wooden table protected by a thick plastic film. I gladly ignore grown-up conversation about family drama, focusing instead on stuffing my face with home cooking, smacking my lips a little too loudly. I feel almost mischievously young. Uncles, mothers, fathers, aunties, brothers, sisters, cousins—I pick up bits here and there, this chatter in the flutters of hometown Sindhi I can only half understand, not having grown up here.

Something about Nani being so naïve as to give away her bangles whenever someone asked her for a loan. Another bit about how Apa Jan would leave black-and-blue marks on your thigh if you left the *chulo* on. How, at age sixteen, Naseem Babi came to marry Aslam Mamou, who was seventeen years her senior; and how her aunties and her mother prayed after sour-milk promises were made—gripping their *tasbihs* tightly—that Naseem Babi would actually *like* this older man. How the success of this marital fable is revealed in the beginning, because we are sitting here today, right now, happily, as a family. I am half aware of the moral aim of this story, with its awkward empirical dimensions: In Order to Be Happy, One Must Marry *Isma'ili*, Even If It's a Little Creepy. There is a part of me that enjoys—with a notable degree of reservation—this simplified offering of a great, confusing truth.

I am quietly pondering the onset of diabetes during postdinner *kulfi* when my old *chacha* speaks, from the head of the table, in an affected, deep baritone; a man asserting his God-given right to silence and command.

I look up stunned—*Is he talking to me?*—first straight ahead, then left, and then right—to find the collective gaze set upon me. Eyes range from expectant to earnest to curious. And of course, there's Pops's shit-eating grin. I am positive I have melted *kulfi* cream all up in my beard.

"Sorry—what did you ask, *Chacha*?"

How old are you now—no longer a question but an annoyed test of patience.

It was inevitable. I already knew whatever number I said would precipitate the dangerous mantra my uncle was dead set on delineating. At twenty-nine, this question is a predetermined, existential adjudication: the contextual set of evidence being that my older cousins (all twenty-six of them) are exempt from this line of questioning; that my sister is well on her way toward respectable, *Isma'ili* family-hood; and that here in the old country, my tawdry theories of progressive neocultural hybridization make even less sense than usual. I make eye contact with no one, grab a little Karachi banana from the center spread of postdinner fruits, and brace for the worst.

"You're overdue," he says.

Like rent. Like car payments. Like this banana covered in soft, brown spots.

Across the table, the look on Ma's face is unmistakably one of a mind at work. She is calculating some monstrosity of a multivariable equation, involving my sister's marriage at twenty-five and upcoming five-year anniversary; twenty-six weddings of twenty-six first cousins; three grandnieces and four grandnephews; thirty-seven years of marriage to Pops—such that in the multifarious matrix of time, tradition, and propriety, all tallies end up with me in the red: overdue.

Paola's Infinite Street Cred

Sofiya's eyes are a little sunken, and up close, nose-to-nose—her breath mixing with my own—they are vast. The darkness of her eyes against the light brown of her cheeks makes it seem as if she was born with a just-right touch of kohl in permanent, perfect placement. I can't see it, but her smile reverberates up through the delicate folds of her cheek under her eyes; her nose is soft as it slides across the side of my own; our eyes close gently, slowly, and into the moment.

Four days before, Paola and I were taking a Tuesday postwork stroll around the municipal lake. She noticed I'd stopped paying attention to her workday story, and that moreover, our easy gait was accelerating toward a light jog. My eyes were trained fifty feet ahead of us on a certain striking somebody. Paola, being my lifelong best friend, could see right through me.

"Do you know her or something?"

"What? Oh yeah, maybe—I think she goes to my *masjid*."

"Oh shit, really?"

I begged her to slow down as she began to tear ass toward the Unidentified Potentially *Isma'ili Chokri*. Paola knew what it meant—she had known my mother too long *not* to—that meeting a UPIC in an unprovoked, real-world, love-interest-type situation had all the trimmings of a big deal.

I pulled at her arm, but she broke my tackle: either she was looking to score eternal street cred with Ma, or else Paola's rambunctious streak was some uncashed check of childhood revenge. Regardless, it was no more than a minute later that I was taking a first shy glance into Sofiya's eyes.

"Hello."

Game Recognize Antigame

It is undeniable that at its foundation, Pops's *jamat khana* status as a Sweet & Funny Uncle is built upon merciless flirtation. It's kind enough, and seemingly aimed at no particular gender, so as not to cross the line to Creepy Uncle. Pops makes it hard to not love him, a cup of Bapa Uncle's chai in one hand, the other busied by gesticulation; holding court with his old buddies, or the twentysomething Corporate-Type IndoPaks who live in the city, or maybe the East Bay young college students. They are always laughing.

My sister Zarah either occupies her own group, or plays a perfect second fiddle to Pops's irresistible charm—she is gregarious, attentive, kind, and a little sassy. *Dynamic* even. Her laugh can warm hearts and capture souls—as it's done with Samir, my incredibly handsome but awkward brother-in-law; a caring being, yes, but one who will often wait in the parking lot to avoid conversation.

Ma operates on a more prophetic plane inside the prayer hall— if the game isn't spiritual, she's probably not playing it—or else, it's the kind of fastidious social-religious work that would seemingly require a clipboard. (She doesn't need one, though. Her practical capacity for doing good by her fellow *murids* is only surpassed by her spiritual one.)

Let's say now—for the sake of experimentation—that one Friday, I happen to notice a Striking Woman by Bapa's chai percolator.

If you've been keeping score, things, seemingly, should go my way: sister and Pops, clever and engaging, masters of flirtation—are well occupied by their respective crowds. My handsome brother-in-law waves timidly while backing toward the door. My mother is either in a corner of the prayer hall, still silent and rocking at a Sufi's pace, or else doing good somewhere.

Taking advantage of the moment, I move toward the percolator, mindlessly busy myself with chai preparation, and maybe get out a quick and mellow "hello" to said Striking Woman—the one and only innocent second before the Avalanche begins. Oh, my dear SW, let me introduce my entourage of misguided matchmakers: sister-and-Pops, suddenly and inexplicably free, materialize out of thin air, armed with coquettish collocations in stereo sound; brother-in-law Samir lingers awkwardly on the outskirts, having forgotten the keys to the car in my sister's purse; Ma comes over for chai and unassumingly requests full contact information for the *Jamati* database. *Et voilà*—the Avalanche has swallowed me and Striking Woman whole, and I realize, in paralyzed awe, that this is most certainly the death of cool.

An Awkward Proclamation

Ice rattling in glasses, sitting closer than the bar's seat requires—a good first date, yes, but on the edge of something bigger and unspoken: our special *-ism* lingers heavily below the light and airy excitement of getting to know each other, having met just four days before, around the lake. Lost in the flying moments of when someone looks at you like *that*, the day-and-time strikes me and I take an almost involuntary look at my wristwatch: it is Friday, five till, and my hair is a mess.

I wonder who will mention it first.

I make a firm commitment not to—so as not to ruin the beautiful secularity of this budding romance—and she doesn't bat an eye. I don't think she even knows where *jamat khana*, much less Alameda, is. My heart buzzes at this possibility; then, on the bar, so does my iPhone: *MA* in big letters, visible to both of us.

"BABA, IT'S ALMOST DUA TIME! ARE YOU COMING?"

She always screams into cell phones. I turn down the volume in the earpiece and shoot a nervous smile toward Sofiya, who thinks either that this is cute, or that I am not the grown-ass man I purport to be. I hope for the former.

I let Ma down gently, all the while knowing that if she really knew what I was doing—exchanging loose looks with *not-just-any-chokri*—missing Friday *dua* would be the kind of spiritual sacrifice that this particular Daughter of Abraham would offer up without a second thought. When I put the phone down, Sofiya's eyes have that look of, *So are you going to say it or am I?*

And out it comes, in all its awkward glory:

"So . . . we are *Isma'ili.*"

" . . . "

"It was my mom, it's *dua* time . . . I mean, you know."

I decide that her silence says enough, that, yes, she does *know*, not just that it's *dua* time, but that there are several parallel dimensions of time at work: it is overdue-*shadi* time; it is we're-not-getting-any-younger-cultural-wish-fulfillment time; it's jeez-it's-nice-being-on-a-date-not-set-up-by-my-auntie time; it's holy-shit-you're-*Isma'ili*-and-I-like-you-I-wonder-if-my-parents-were-right time.

A few hours later, nose-to-nose, she tells me, in the dreamy almost of a whisper, that she can't believe I'm *Isma'ili.* I take a page out of her book and keep my exclamations inside. *I* can't believe that the only thing compelling this tender moment is volition, that I am *choosing* to be nasally close, that the *-ism* is absent, and the perfect storm of sister-and-Pops, brother, and Ma aren't watching from somewhere, leaning in with their good-natured, poorly-executed yenta-ing.

Waiting for the Death of Everyone

"Baba, you will finish your master's, then get a good job, and then you will meet a nice *Isma'ili chokri.* . . . I mean, Baba, you're over . . ."

Due. Yeah, I know.

My mother's zealous embrace of Old Chacha's Mantra for Yours Truly is so unimaginatively textbook that I find the tired Ghosts of Every Pakistani Immigrant Past—the scenes in which a young brown boy has to explain, unintelligibly, why he neatly stacks pepperoni in the corner of his post-soccer-game paper plate; why root beer would cause some very understandable confusion; what a *masjid*, no less a *jamat khana*, is and why he keeps missing Friday-night school dances—are resurrected and renewed with each incantation of the O-word.

I thought, in the case of my family, as the *Pakistani* continues its steady, two-score drift toward the *Pakistan American*—cue Pops's frustrating assimilatory rhetoric about "The Greatest Nation on Earth" and "Democracy and Freedom"—that these weary Ghosts would finally get some deserved rest. That maybe, in their place, we would build new, complex, and nuanced stories, alive and reflective of our changing conditions; that our stories would engender the myths, morals, and lore that shall trickle down and guide posterity.

I guess not.

Instead, I am now abruptly exposed to this redoubled effort for cultural continuity and core value, after hiding, for the past half decade, in the penumbra of my sister's wedding. Zarah, true to traditional form, got married at twenty-five—not just to some man with subcontinental roots—but a bona fide, Allah-fearin', Ali-lovin' *Shia Imami Isma'ili* Muslim. She kept not only in the race *but in the sect!*

This choice deserves no reprehension—excuse me if I've made it sound so. I respect the values and honor the deep love hidden in my mother's hackneyed proclamations. Moreover, I witness, almost daily, the ease, joy, and love in my sister's marriage. This is *the* ease, the very same brand of it, that my parents have fought their uphill, immigrant fights to secure for *me*. Shit, maybe I'm even a little envious about how things have worked out for my sister. What is this obscure desire for Freedom and Democracy in my love life? Is this—*gasp*—what assimilation feels like?

I used to joke with my cousins about how we just needed to wait until the entire parent generation dies before the work of neo-*Isma'ilism* can commence. Seems like I'm the only one who still remembers the joke.

Ha.

The Deathblow

Paola sometimes does this thing where she mouths the words you're saying while you're talking to her, somewhere between repetition and prediction, so it kind of looks like she's a mirror that's trying to read your mind. This is especially the case after coming home from a date, when the action potential of a kiss-and-tell story takes her into full-steam predictive mode: she'll even start dropping the occasional sentence finisher or two.

It's Monday evening, I didn't see Paola all weekend; the anticipation has reached a boil. So when I start telling her about the peculiar last few days re: Sofiya—a record of cosmic oddities and bad luck in the gauzy shadow of a phenomenal first date—her penchant for prediction ends up becoming the proverbial last straw:

"Many things, P. A few too many bad omens with this one. Weird shit. I mean she's fantastic, but—"

"—she looks like your sister?"

" . . . "

The innocence of it and the honesty behind it soften the blow a bit, but *goddamn it*—this is never something anyone wants to hear.

Although unintentional, Paola's unfortunate proclivity for sentence closers was the masterstroke at the end of a brief and ill-fated potential love-interest-type situation, a fitting capstone to a weekend of madness and misfortune. Suddenly, my special Friday night feelings couldn't have seemed further away, and I was left in wonderment: how could it all fall to pieces in seventy-two hours?

Summer Camp Buddies

So I tell Paola everything.

I tell her about how I went to sleep on Friday reeling in the nuances of a date at once volitional and votive, strange and intimate. And how I slept soundly, grinning like a dope.

Then, a rude awakening: on a clear and bright Saturday morning—the morning after an outstanding first date—the unseasonable, the unpredictable, the damn near impossible for such a low altitude: the Avalanche.

A Saturday morning text message from *ZARAH* read: *Heard you had a big date last night ;) LOL.*

With the speed afforded only by modern smartphone technology, I dialed my sister's number with the kind of panicked instinct expressly reserved for autonomic processes. My mind caught up a half second later and I ended the call to assess: How? Who? Paola? No, impossible. Public place—spying? *Allah?*

I call back another minute later, and my sister answered the phone with a kind of elongated *hey*, stretched out extra long in that I-know-what-you-did-last-night kind of tone. I cursed at her immediately in a half-playful, half-sororicidal fashion, demanding truth and explanations.

The taqueria. They met in line. We had just *talked* about this specific taqueria, the night before—how I love it, how Sofiya loves it, how the whole fam loves it—did I put it in her head?

"Your *friend* happens to know Samir—they went to Al-Ummah together, in '96."

I was beyond belief. Zarah knew this, and I sensed she was graciously holding back her pleasure at my suffering. *Isma'ili* summer camp? Upstate New York? Fifteen years ago?

"What's the damage?"

"Me, Samir—Pops was there, too. Don't worry, we've already agreed not to tell Mom."

She read my mind. This was bad enough. Definitely can't tell Ma. Things were already turning for the worse. Telling Ma would introduce a wild card into an already fragile situation. The explosive potential energy of mentioning The Fabled *Isma'ili Chokri* could very well blow this whole thing apart.

On the phone with my sister still, the call-waiting screen popped up, reading SOFIYA. I took a deep breath, but not deep enough, and inadvertently answered with that same stupid *hey* my sister had just used.

Cosmic Kismet

So it's not as bad I think: Zarah and Pops kept it cool, and apparently Samir, in a rare case of animation—brought on, perhaps, by fond camp memories—was a bit charming himself. The worst of it is in my head, as the soul search for The Meaning of All This commences: is this a simple coincidence? A cute cosmic joke? Foul play, or maybe conspiracy? More than anything, where can I find some privacy in the -*ism*? Is that even possible, or else, the point? I feel an acute sense of dread: the shrinking space of my formerly independent potential love-interest-type situation.

The coup de grâce à la Paola, of course, would become the-end-as-we-know-it of this hapless love, but it was truly the irony of Ma's sense of spiritual-religious responsibility that set everything in motion toward an irrevocable end: a mundane Sunday closet-cleaning, a phone number found, remembrance of a promise, and a love-shattering phone call.

I imagine it sounded something like this:

"Hello, is this Sofiya? *Ya Ali madad*, darling, my name is Sha-mim Aunty, from Alameda *jamat khana*. How are you doing? . . .

Good, *beta*. Well, Sofiya honey, I met your mother a few months ago . . . Yes, right, when she was visiting. She gave me your number and I've just now found it . . . I know, funny . . . Well, she said that you might need a reminder every now and again to come to *jamat khana*, and I promised her I would call you, so darling, you should really try to make it some Friday . . . Mmhmm, yes, I know . . . mmhmm . . . of course. You live where? Oh perfect! My son lives in Oakland, he has a car, his name is—"

Again, *SOFIYA*—a text this time—which reads, thirty-six hours after Friday night: *I think your mother just called me.*

Bapa's Chai

Navroz always packs the house—a fire hazard of a Persian New Year celebration, where 130 *murids* squeeze into the tiny office-park-cum-*masjid*, capacity 70. I know she'll be there, and I consider joining Samir in the parking lot to sit this one out. We hadn't spoken in weeks, vis-à-vis my precipitous drop off the planet. Just thinking about the bullshit sincerity of the clichéd excuse—*I'm just not in that place right now*, or *You're just too good*, or the immortal *I don't want to get attached*—was making me sick with anxiety. To lie so unabashedly, and to cloak it in earnestness: it seems almost sacrilegious to wield such *dunya* banalities in a place so expressly concerned with cultivating a healthy sense of *deen*.

She's standing right by Bapa's percolator, and moving in this time elicits no familial Avalanche (their absence most likely spurred by a fiery tirade at the dinner table on the topic of "Minding One's Own Business," by Yours Truly). We get some air outside, the steam of our chais rising from Styrofoam cups into the cool March night. Behind the strained, excruciatingly robotic small talk, Sofiya's eyes are calling: *So are you going to say it, or am I?*

I want to say it all, I want to paint a picture of my mental land-scape so vivid that it would surely rescue me from my current (presumed) status as Another Asshole Who Didn't Call. I want to tell her about how I can't deal with the ways in which the *-ism* looms so large. That I want to stand up from prostration and speak directly into the big, scary face of Tradition, and say, *Hey, bow toward me a little bit, like I bow toward you!* Just give me some room, and I'll do this my way, and I'll do it with good heart and a right mind, like you taught me! But is this really a conversation to have with an institution? Or is it a really about my mother? As in Ma, I love you, but I'm a grown-ass man and you can't play a major part in my love life, albeit by utter cosmic accident.

So I don't: I don't say any of it. My heart and mind go cold like this chai in my hands, and I spout off some spurious excuse-for-an-excuse that impresses no one and leaves both of us feeling ashamed and sad.

I slink back through the front door of the office-park-cum-*masjid*, into the warmth of bodies created by endless uncles and aunties standing too close to one another; into the warmth of knowing that Ma and Pops and Zarah and Samir—abashed and perhaps afraid of me for tonight—linger somewhere out of my line of sight; into the warmth of Bapa's gaze, who signals to me, sticks his finger into my cold chai, shoots me an indignant glance before he dumps it out, and pours me a hot, fresh cup.

Who I Needed to Be

By Yusef Ramelize

The day I lost my virginity it was hot and humid. The inside of the one-bedroom, fourth-floor apartment felt like a sauna. It was dark and my face was wet with sweat as she began kissing places that hadn't been kissed before. I could taste the sweat on her neck when I kissed her back. The salty taste made me want to throw up. I hesitated, but then continued, curiosity and desire surpassing my wanting to stop. She took a condom out of her dress pocket. I could tell she was experienced and was surprised by how much she wanted me.

We met at the beauty salon where I had my first full-time job, as a barber. The salon was located in a rough part of Brooklyn, New York. I was just out of high school and she was the twenty-one-year-old aunt of one of my regular clients, a seven-year-old boy. She was always well dressed and seemed kind and friendly in our brief conversations. In addition to our usual pleasantries, she made flirtatious comments hinting at her interest.

"Yusef, you have such nice eyes!" she'd say as I smiled bashfully. "I love our conversations, we should hang out sometime."

A few weeks later, I took her up on her offer and invited her over to my mother's apartment after my mother left for work. After only a few minutes and sentences we ended up on the kitchen floor.

My pants were around my ankles. I was curious and felt I had gone too far to stop. Each breath she took was long and passionate. She bit me on my neck and my ear. Then, in a flash, it was all over. I froze. She was talking to me, but everything sounded garbled and distant. It hit me. I had lost my virginity.

I was completely overcome with guilt and shame. I pushed away from her and ran into the bathroom. I went to the sink to make *wudu* and immediately dropped to my knees in prostration, begging God for forgiveness. "*Bismillah al-Rahman al-Rahim*," I said. I recited every prayer I knew, bowing, prostrating with my hands raised toward the sky. When I glanced back, I saw an extremely confused look on her face. She put on her clothes without saying a word and walked out. That was the last time I ever saw her. I had neglected to tell her two things: I was a virgin and I was a Muslim.

I hadn't thought those two things would matter. But losing my virginity to someone I didn't love and to whom I wasn't married made me feel empty. That day, I realized how deep my faith ran and glimpsed the importance of love before intimacy.

Growing up, there weren't a lot of conversations about love or sex in my household. My family shaped my first messages about love during my childhood, and my father had the biggest influence on me.

When I was younger, I wanted my father to show me affection to prove that he cared for me. I don't remember him ever giving me a hug. I don't remember him telling me that he loved me. He owned several businesses, and worked a lot, so we rarely spent time together. What I remember of our time together is mainly beatings, punishments, and fear.

One of my most painful memories occurred when I was seven. My father was extremely upset after my sibling accused me of doing something I hadn't done. He burst into the bathroom while I was taking a bath.

"How many times have I told you not to come into my bedroom without asking!" he shouted.

"I didn't, Abu! I wasn't in your room." I cried.

He was furious. Every time I declared my innocence it made him even angrier. He dragged me out of the bathtub by my hands. The water dripped from my skin, leaving a sudsy trail down the hallway.

I was screaming, trying to get loose, but my father's grip was too strong to break. He dragged me into his bedroom and grabbed the nearest belt. There was never a shortage of belts around the house, as much as I tried to hide them. He held me up in the air with one hand and beat me until his arm was tired.

Then there was the emotional neglect. It made me feel like I was invisible to my father and, eventually, to everyone else around me. Nothing I did mattered or could make a difference. I was angry, full of hatred, and emotionally detached. Because I thought my father didn't love me, it was hard for me to love him.

My father died of prostate cancer in 1992, when I was fourteen. In his last few hours on earth I didn't stay by his bedside to say a prayer. I didn't hold his hand before his last breath. Instead, I was in the next room wishing he had shown me the love I'd always wanted. I couldn't let go of the pain of having a father who didn't love me even while he grasped for life.

Grieving friends and relatives traveled from all over to say their final good-byes at my father's funeral. Yet, as one of his three sons, I just couldn't find the love in my heart to fully mourn. Tears filled everyone's eyes around me, but I couldn't let go of all the hurt inside.

After my father died, I moved from Trinidad to Brooklyn, to live with my mother. It wasn't until I was sixteen—two years after my father passed away—that his death hit me. I dreamt I was running from someone, but I couldn't see his face. My heart was pounding. The faster I ran, the faster the person behind me ran. Just when I thought I had gotten away, the road ended and I fell off a steep cliff. As I went over the edge, someone grabbed my hand and pulled me back up onto steady ground. At first I couldn't see the person's face, but as he pulled me closer, I saw that it was my father.

I woke up in a cold sweat. The grief finally hit. I started crying that morning and didn't stop until sunset. My eyes were bloodshot and I ended up missing the whole day of school.

When my mom came home from work, I told her about the dream. This wasn't the first time we had spoken about my relationship with my father, but speaking with her that day helped me to understand things about Abu that before that moment I hadn't been ready to accept.

"Sometimes a father's love goes way beyond the words and the things that his children might see," my mom said with tears in her eyes. "Everyone has a different way of expressing love. Of course, some ways are healthier than others, but sometimes parents repeat what they learned from their life experiences and struggles. That doesn't mean that your father didn't love you."

I thought deeply about all the things my mom said, the things my father did and didn't do, who he was and who he wasn't. It helped me to realize that though my father hadn't loved me the way I wanted him to, he had loved me in the best way he could. I couldn't condone all he had done, but I decided to let go of the fear and pain that had held me back for so long.

By accepting my father, I began my journey toward understanding love. In order to satisfy my curiosity about women, sex, and love, I had turned to TV, movies, magazines, and videos. But these things had given me an incomplete view of love. After I lost my virginity on that kitchen floor, I didn't feel satisfied, enlightened, or loved. There was something missing. I realized that my life was full of fear—fear of failing, of not being good enough, and of not being worthy of love. I questioned everything, how I talked, looked, even how I stood. This insecurity affected most of my romantic relationships. I had asked myself why women didn't love me but never once questioned why I didn't love myself.

This realization was a turning point for me. I needed to clear my own path toward a relationship and toward Islam. My biggest challenge in my relationships with women was the contradictory expectations I had of them. This was most true in the area of religion, where I wanted Muslim women at times to behave like non-Muslims and was disappointed when non-Muslim women didn't behave like Muslims. I needed to shift my focus, and started by asking myself, Who do *I* need to be in order to meet and attract the person that I'm looking for?

As a first step, I knew I had to improve my practice of Islam. I began by seeking a community where I could build a network of Muslim friends who could help me progress with my *deen*. Although I attended *Jumma* regularly, and had bounced around to different mosques, I had never found a community where I felt comfortable. One Ramadan, while attending Friday prayers, a friend reminded me about the importance of the last ten days of the holy month. He suggested that I attend *tarawih* at the Islamic center on Ninety-Sixth Street in Manhattan. So on the twenty-seventh night, I stood in prayer from dusk until dawn.

Even though we had prayed all through the night until the morning prayer, I wasn't tired. This was the first time I had experienced something so exhilarating and transporting. I felt so connected to God and grateful for what He had provided. The sun had just risen and it was time to head home. While I was waiting for the train, I saw a group of Muslims on the platform who had also just come from the mosque. We entered the same subway car and I joined their conversation. They were members of the Islamic center at New York University, and they introduced me to the community I had been searching for, one that was accepting, compassionate, and understanding. They opened their doors to me when I needed it most and created a learning environment for everyone regardless of their degree of religious practice. This was a space in which I knew I could grow.

Eventually, with a new outlook, new connection with God, and new community to support me, I finally felt ready to find my mate. Now, in my late twenties, I wasn't looking for a girlfriend or something merely sexual. I was ready for marriage and wanted to connect with someone who was Muslim and wanted the same. Meeting my wife, then, wasn't just a matter of time or circumstance; it was a part of process that had begun when I was a teenager.

I met Samira on a Facebook group page called the African American Muslim Marriage Connection. A Muslim couple had started the page in hopes of connecting Muslims who were seriously looking for a partner. After a couple of months and a few failed connections, I saw a picture of a young *hijabi* with a gorgeous smile. She seemed happy, pleasant, and approachable. We shared similar backgrounds: both of us were African Americans from big New York families, were raised Muslim, and enjoyed Caribbean music and dancing.

What gave me major pause was that even though she was originally from nearby Harlem, she was living in Muscat, Oman. I was living in Queens, and there was an eight-hour time difference and more than seven thousand miles between us. My previous experiences with long-distance relationships had been bad and I'd vowed never again to consider someone who wasn't in the same area as me. But something about her smile finally made me reach out.

I "friended" her and sent a simple message introducing myself. We started with short e-mails, which eventually turned into really long e-mails. After some time we started Skyping. Our connection was unlike any I'd experienced before. She had all the qualities that I'd mentally listed as desirable in a spouse, down to the little, silly things. Our conversations felt so natural, like I could tell her anything—and I did! To work around the time difference, I would get up at *fajr* and be with her all morning while she finished praying *isha* and wound down her day. We would often watch each other fall asleep on Skype, not wanting to miss a second of each other's lives.

After a few months of sleepless nights and daily communications, she told me she was returning to New York for her sister's wedding. I took that week off from work so that I could be available whenever she had a free moment. When I received the text that she'd arrived, I was overwhelmed with excitement and nerves.

After months of talking on the phone I was going to finally meet the woman who had captured my heart from seven thousand miles away. I had everything planned: a lovely brunch at Sugar Cane—one of my favorite Caribbean restaurants—in Park Slope, a romantic stroll in the Brooklyn Botanic Garden, followed by a trip to Max Brenner, one of the best chocolate spots in Manhattan. As I was parking I got her text, "I'm here :)." This was it.

I crossed the street to the restaurant and saw her waiting in front. All I could think about was how I wanted to hug her and not let go, but I wanted to make a good, halal first impression. So I greeted her and let her make the first move. She gave me a quick hug and we stared at each other for a few seconds, both in awe of seeing the other in person.

Unfortunately, the restaurant was closed. I started to panic a little, but suggested that we walk to another restaurant two blocks away. I was so enraptured that I took us in the wrong direction. Six blocks later, she pointed to an Italian bistro with nice outdoor seating: "Is that the restaurant you were talking about it?"

I had no idea where I was.

"Yup, that's it!" I said, relieved that I didn't have to admit I was lost.

As we sat across from each other, I was mesmerized by her beautiful brown complexion. It was easy to see her tan from the desert sun in Oman. After we finished eating we were ready to head to the second part of our day at the botanic garden. As we approached the entrance of the garden, I could see a big "CLOSED" sign from halfway down the block. "You've got to be kidding me!" I thought to myself. The garden was closed for a private event. Strike two.

I could feel the panic rising again. But Samira suggested that we take a stroll through Prospect Park instead. We ended up lying on the grass looking up at the sky, talking and listening to music from the same headphones for hours. I was relaxed and comfortable. Before I knew it, it was five o'clock. She was already late for a meeting with her sister, so we had to cancel the chocolate dessert.

With each of my planned events having failed, I turned to her and asked, "How could a day go so wrong yet feel so great?" It *had* been a perfect day and we were sad to see it end. We hugged, and parted with salaams.

That week remains one of the best weeks of my life. Day after day I became more excited and more sure that this was the person I wanted to spend the rest of my life with. What surprised me was that my certainty didn't come from my being in love with her. Instead, it stemmed from my knowing what I wanted and knowing I was ready for it. Samira had all of the qualities I'd been looking for in a partner. She made me laugh, she was patient and humble, and she made me feel like she would always be there for me, no matter what. These were the qualities that mattered most; the qualities I strove for in myself and looked for in the person I wanted to commit to for the rest of my life.

Samira decided to move back to New York City permanently after we both realized that we were utterly and undeniably in love. We got married on December 31, 2011. When I look at my wife, I think about all of the things I went through to get here, to her. As much shame as I felt for years of living contrary to Islamic norms, I don't have any regrets. Everything I experienced helped me become who I am today and who I needed to be for her to enter my life. My struggles with faith and failures in relationships helped me identify the qualities I wanted in a spouse. They helped me to appreciate unconditional love and reciprocate that love when God granted it to me.

An Unlikely Foe

By Yousef Turshani

This is the story of a mama's boy who falls in love with a good girl and brings her home to meet his parents.

Except that I'm not a perfect mama's boy and this is the fourth girl I've brought home in just over five years.

Postcollege life can be tough for a young Muslim in America, especially for a cross-country transplant coming out of a strong Muslim Student Association. It's not easy to meet other twenty-somethings. That's why, as a new resident at the UCLA children's hospital, I found MECA, a social group for Muslims in Southern California, like a group of friends waiting to pop out of a package shouting, "Tear here!"

It's a cool autumn evening in 2007 at a gorgeous home in LA where about a hundred of us are gathered for our monthly potluck, this time celebrating the end of Ramadan. The kitchen is abuzz with conversation while children and adults grab their plates, mouths watering at the smells and sights of curry, *shawarma*, and stews, as well as the moist cookies and chocolate frosting.

I hand a plate to Taz before grabbing my own. It's great to have a fellow punk rocker activist in our crew. We talk about upcoming shows in SoCal. And when she asks where we should sit, I suggest a table outside, where I spot some new faces.

At the end of the table three UC Davis friends are catching up. Sema and Aysha are both in grad school close by. Nadeah has just returned after traveling the world for a year and is living at home an hour away in Irvine, looking for jobs.

As people finish their food and mill around, Nadeah and I walk around the pool, side-stepping kids' floaties as she tells me about visiting Pondicherry, India, where her mom grew up. We compare the crazy traffic of Egypt, where she lived for a few months with her best friend, with that in my parents' native Libya, where I spent a handful of my childhood summers. Egypt definitely takes the cake.

My crew is ready for the postpotluck gathering. Sev—our Polish, Muslim-convert, hedge-fund-trader friend—offers up his swanky Brentwood apartment. I invite the Davis trio to join us, but they get lost. When they finally arrive, the evening is winding down, but I make sure to exchange numbers with the two women who live close by. It feels a bit forward to ask for Nadeah's digits given that she lives an hour away. Besides, I sense that I'll see her again, as she'll be coming up to hang out with her friends.

Sure enough, we meet up a few more times that first month. At Knott's Scary Farm, I ride one too many roller coasters in a row and lean on Nadeah for support. She tells me about her passion for international human rights and her desire to be an activist on behalf of the underserved. I mention my summers spent with Volunteers for Peace in Spain, Iceland, and Scotland, or surveying community health workers in Nicaragua.

It's invigorating to meet a like-minded young Muslim. Someone not only willing to head to strange lands to serve God by helping the less fortunate, but motivated to make a career out of it. She shares my view of Islam—a faith that commands us to learn about cultures and languages different from our own, to gain knowledge and skills so we can put them to use for the benefit of humanity. Even if nothing romantic emerges, I find myself thinking, we can support each other in our endeavors as friends.

When my top-choice residency in San Francisco has an open spot and offers me an interview, it seems that friends is all we may ever be. I'm thrilled about the interview, but wonder about us. Although

Nadeah and I met less than a month ago, I feel a mature connection to her. Beyond her striking beauty and comforting nature, our shared values point to the possibility of something real between us. I've dreamed of meeting a woman like her.

My best friends like to tease me that I fall hard and quick for girls. I'd wanted my previous long-term relationships to work out so much that I ignored obvious flaws: the Colombian convert who wanted to settle down while we were teenagers; the Syrian professor who didn't want to live anywhere but Chicago; and the Italian psychologist who was unfaithful to me. It wasn't until my parents brought up unrelated objections to each woman that I allowed myself to step back and see the problems.

I decide to tell Nadeah about my interview, but before I begin she says, "I got a job interview to be a field representative for a California assemblywoman! I'm so excited!"

"Congratulations! What area does this assemblywoman represent?" I ask.

"In the San Francisco Bay Area," she replies.

"No way! I have an interview in San Francisco next week," I tell her.

"Me too! How were you planning on going up there? I was thinking of driving up on Friday and making a weekend out of it," she says.

"Me too! So, umm, maybe we could drive up together? Save the environment?" I ask, smiling as she agrees.

Our love blossoms over the next six months, as we commute most weekends to see each other on either side of the bay. During this time, she applies to law school. One day, while I'm boarding a plane to Italy to visit extended family, she calls to let me know she's been accepted to a school in the Midwest.

"They offered me an international law fellowship. That is *exactly* why I want to go to law school! The catch is, I have to accept it within a week. Yousef, I know you're about to leave for a couple of weeks so I'm glad I caught you. Do you have any thoughts?" Nadeah asks.

I take a deep breath, feeling the weight of this moment. It's a major life decision and she's reaching out to ask my opinion. It'll be tough to be three time zones apart, especially while both of us are working and studying hard. But at the core of our relationship is the value of supporting each other's dreams.

"Nadeah, I'm so happy for you! If this is the best decision for your future, go for it. We'll figure things out." The flight attendant asks me to turn off my phone, cutting off further discussion.

That summer Nadeah, her father, and I pack up her apartment and drive across the country in her overfilled Civic. In October, on the first anniversary of the day we met, she flies to San Francisco for a long weekend. I take her to a spot she's never been—the top of Buena Vista Park. It's a special place for me because, during the six months she lived in Hayward, I would climb up the hill to look across the bay, knowing she was working on the other side.

While she is taking in the view, her mother calls. I quickly hand my camera to a sunbathing stranger and reach into my pocket for the ring. After Nadeah hangs up the phone and turns toward me, I go down on bended knee and look into those eyes that I have so often found myself swimming in, not wanting to come up for a breath.

Tears begin rolling down her face as I ask her to marry me. We are elated to be engaged and have no clue of the looming challenges that will rip us apart.

My parents both grew up on the Mediterranean Sea, in Tripoli, Libya. My mom's father was a fisherman. My mother and her siblings often went out on the boat with him on weekends. He'd cast a large net into the open sea and they'd eagerly jump into the deep blue, hoisting the day's catch.

My dad was a jock who played two to three hours of soccer or basketball most afternoons. When close enough to the beach, he'd swim out into the ocean until his arms got tired and just float—face soaked by the sun, in saltwater so buoyant he could even fall asleep.

Their idyllic life was shattered during their teens by the revolution. By the time they married, ten years into Muammar Qaddafi's crippling dictatorship, they knew their beloved homeland was not a suitable place to raise their children. My father whisked my mother—who had been beyond Libya's borders only twice before, to visit neighboring Egypt—to the strange state of Kentucky. The language was odd, the winters bitter, and the food unpalatable— with the exception of her new favorite, KFC.

During my mother's pregnancy, her beloved mother died unexpectedly. Fearing for my mother's health, my father and her sisters decided it best to not tell her until after my birth. Yet she sensed that something was amiss back home. She began having dreams that her mother had died. In these dreams, her mother told her not to worry, for her child would soothe her sorrow.

Her intense attachment to me sustained her through the 1980s, when travel to see our extended family in Libya was impossible. As a senior in high school, I was a member of the varsity wrestling team. The one and only time she watched a match, I was thrown onto the mat by a stronger opponent. She instinctively got up, ran down the aisle of the gymnasium seeking to rip my opponent off of me. During my junior year in college, while studying abroad in England, I stored all my belongings at my parents' house. When I returned, I saw that my mother had gone through everything and thrown out love letters and a picture of my then-girlfriend.

Whether the adversary was a wrestler or a girlfriend, she wanted no one to hurt me or take me away from her. It wasn't until I started having serious relationships in college that I realized how dysfunctional her attachment was.

"Yousef, she's just not right. We only want what's best for you, you understand?" my mother said.

"What are you talking about?" I retorted, furious. "We had the engagement party a month ago and you seemed happy with Nadeah, her parents, and the arrangements."

"They are very nice; they took good care of us, *habibi*. But something is just too different. They may be too traditional for us. They want to do things like in India at the wedding, but we are not from there. How are your kids going to be raised? Are they even going to speak Arabic?"

She went on to demand that I end the relationship, saying they'd never accept Nadeah as their daughter.

Her grasping-at-straws excuses were becoming all too familiar. As a teen, I'd fiercely created my own identity as an American Muslim. I was a straightedge punk before I knew the term existed. Despite being surrounded by friends who smoked weed or drank alcohol, I felt no need to indulge. By high school, I was crowd-surfing and starting mosh pits at punk shows. I was invigorated by the energy of the crowd and by the lyrics exhorting listeners to speak up against abusive authority and for oppressed minorities. The punk ethic of social justice was rooted in my understanding of Islam.

Also rooted in my understanding of Islam: the tenet of obeying and seeking the advice of one's mother.

Each time I'd been in a serious relationship, I wanted to include my parents. They accepted that I wasn't eager to be "set up" with a family friend, as is the norm in Libya. They didn't want to show up on the wedding day to accept complete strangers into our family either. Yet, each time I introduced them to a woman, they had complaints about her that seemed arbitrary or unfounded.

Nadeah and I transformed from giddy fiancés into a bickering couple. She'd descended into the never-ending winter of her Cleveland law school; I had eighty-hour weeks of pediatric intensive care in San Francisco. This didn't leave much time for listening to each other's woes, let alone dealing with two increasingly disillusioned sets of parents living in different parts of the country.

I was in the on-call room during a twenty-four-hour shift when I got Nadeah's phone call.

"Yousef, I just can't do this anymore. I can't marry into a family that rejects me with a husband who won't stand up for me. I love you so much and wanted this to work, but I can't even think straight anymore. I'll always love you, but unless something changes, I have to focus on law school. I feel so sad already," she trailed off before hanging up.

The on-call room suddenly resembled a prison cell—even more than it usually did. I felt as though I'd been sentenced to a life of arduous around-the-clock shifts and repeated heartbreaks. My fiancée was being ripped away from me and all I could do was cry. I was numb and lost without her in my life. It took a few weeks of wallowing in self-pity before I could take the initiative to win her back.

The following month, Nadeah was flying home to Irvine for spring break. I had only one weekend off that month and made sure it coincided with her visit. My intention was to fly down and somehow win over not only Nadeah, but also her parents. Without a definite plan, I boarded the plane and began scrawling notes on the back of a pediatric journal.

Ringing her doorbell after my arrival, I tried to calm my shaking hands. Her father led me to the living room. I took a deep breath and shared my plan with Nadeah and her parents. A few nods and stipulations later, we agreed that my parents could not disrespect Nadeah again and that they needed to openly accept her before we moved forward.

This hurdle cleared, I had a more stubborn challenge ahead. I had to cut the psychological umbilical cord between my mother and me for good.

My mom still called each week, but I remained distant, reiterating my wish that she accept Nadeah. These were the most strained months I have ever experienced with my parents, our conversations often descending into yelling and hang-ups.

It would take a dream to finally soften her heart.

It was my first time home to Florida, where my parents now lived, in a year. We sat on the couch, looking out onto the inlet watching the dolphins jump.

She looked into my eyes and, with tears glistening on her cheeks, said, "Yousef, you're my only son. You and your sister, Sara, are my everything—the air I breathe. I only wanted what's best for you. I don't want to fight with you anymore. Nadeah came to me in a dream; she held my hand and we walked together to a brightly lit field. I felt such a peace with her."

She paused to reach for tissues.

"I now know that Nadeah will be good for you and for us as a family. I know I'm going to love her like I do my own daughter."

It was Ramadan—a time for forgiveness and mending broken relationships. The month of fasting had given her the chance to realize that she'd been selfish. We stood up and hugged, both wiping away tears. In that moment I understood that I'd gone from being an adolescent to becoming a man. A man who stood up for the woman he loved to the most stubborn and unusual of foes—his own mother.

Nadeah and I married with the blessings of our families a year later. We stood on a naked bluff in Malibu overlooking the Pacific Ocean and said our vows, knowing we'd soon be parted again. Nadeah had landed a prestigious externship at The Hague. She was going to join the first team to prosecute an African head of state for crimes against humanity for the mining of "blood diamonds." Simultaneously, I'd enlisted in Doctors Without Borders for a year, as part of the team managing the largest pediatric HIV center in Zimbabwe.

We were going to continue living our core values of supporting each other's ambitions and aspiring to serve humanity, apart, for now. But, on our wedding night, we danced until late with our parents and our friends, embracing each other—eager for the adventures that lay ahead.

A Pair of Photos

By Ahmed Ali Akbar

I. A Love Story, 1975

The day before they fly to America, Chacha and Raani marry in the living room of Raani's childhood home. The party is small by Pakistani standards—perhaps twenty-five people. Of fiery, brave Raani's family, the core is in attendance. The two junior sisters hover in plain shalwar kameez, colored *dupattas* thrown hastily over their shoulders. The two boys lumber in the corner, hands in trousers. It is a sober affair.

Raani's father had threatened to cancel the wedding. Like many Pakistani men of his generation, he left centuries of tradition post-Partition. Prior to 1947, the majority of his clan had lived near a Sufi shrine in East Punjab. Violent sectarianism scattered that history throughout West Punjab. Given all he had lost, he hoped that his children would marry within the family as he had done. It was improper, he insisted, for Raani, a fine, Urdu-speaking descendent of sheikhs and the clan's first child of Pakistan, to marry a country Punjabi like Chacha. Somehow he acquiesced, perhaps seeing the fire mirrored in his eldest daughter's eyes.

Quiet, loyal Chacha was not so lucky.

His family had also left their land and livelihood in East Punjab. But unlike Raani's scholarly, urban ancestors, they were wealthy rural landowners who married others of their own caste. His sister and each of his five older brothers had married Rajputs of the family's choosing. Chacha did not believe that Islam contained anything like "caste." As the youngest, perhaps he thought he could get his way, but the discussion was short and uncomplicated.

"We do not approve and will not attend."

Chacha did not attempt to convince them. It was the first time he had disobeyed his mother and elder brothers. In a version later told by Raani, Chacha was locked in a bathroom the morning of his wedding, broke out through the window, and took a bus to the ceremony. Chacha laughs and calls it a total fabrication—except for the bus part.

His family boycotts the marriage, including his beloved, widowed mother. Representing the groom's side are three classmates and one of their fathers. All of them will later follow Raani and Chacha to America and become their surrogate family.

It sounds depressing, but Chacha smiles and laughs in every photo. Raani, unusual for her, looks demure as a bride. She hadn't had time to find an outfit for the wedding and wears a red *lehnga* from a recent *Eid*, adorned with her mother's finest gold jewelry.

In Pakistan, a distinction is made between love marriages and arranged ones. Chacha and Raani did not have an arranged marriage but when asked why they married, their answer does not mention love. Instead:

"We were partners."

They met during medical school in Lahore. Chacha's older brothers were of different professions—engineer, politician, diplomat, army man and businessman. Chacha would be his family's first doctor. Raani was following in the footsteps of her mother, an obstetrician. Her sisters and a brother would soon join her in the medical profession. For both, cosmopolitan Lahore represents an unparalleled adventure.

Chacha hangs with a crew of pranksters, the moral compass of the group. There are ten girls in their class of one hundred. Though Raani spends much of her time with those ten, she is the undisputed leader of boys and girls alike. For a long time before their meeting,

Raani hears of a person named Chacha, and she is confused by this name. It means, basically, 'uncle.' She wonders who this Chacha is who could inspire such respect from the male medical students.

When she finally meets him, she is underwhelmed. He is a year her junior. She notices his well-pressed clothes, in contrast to his friends, who lounge around, wearing tank tops and *lungis* and smoking cigarettes. He notices her simple khaddar clothing and asks, "Why are you wearing that clothing?"

"It's for workers' rights. I don't need anything finer than what they spin and wear," she replies. "Here's a better question, *bhai*. Why are you called Chacha?"

He laughs. "You'd have to ask the boys."

"Surely you should know why you have such a strange nickname, Chacha."

"You can just call me Waheed."

"I'm Raani."

Chacha's friends become Raani's friends, and Raani's become Chacha's. As a group, they scribble and share notes, hike in the Himalayan foothills, drink chai and eat *pakoras* at truck stops, mock their professors' English and discuss the unmatchable poetic genius of Faiz Ahmed Faiz. Soon, the boys send food from their mess hall to the girls' dormitory—the girls' *rotis* were stale and their *daal* watery—along with flowers and sweets.

Raani scoffs at the flowers from Chacha, but she is softened by the fact that every time he sends them, he sends a bouquet to her younger sister too. She also finds it strangely endearing that during finals Chacha grows a beard and proceeds to pull hairs from it until a dime-sized hole appears on his chin.

In Chacha, Raani sees someone with competence and a work ethic that can support her revolutionary, feminist ambitions. The two are enamored with the struggle of communist revolutionaries in Latin America and the Muslim world. They debate among their friends the role of Islam in such struggles. Chacha shares the bonds he made with Muslims in Africa and the Middle East, making a convincing argument for Islam's capability to unite.

By the time they graduate, the friends have decided to go to America. The opportunities are better, and anyway, they plan to return—someday. After she graduates from medical school, Raani announces to her father that she is going to America and that she and Chacha want to get married. After a year trying to convince her father, she succeeds. They arrive in snowy New York the day after their marriage.

Initially, there are issues.

Raani is the epitome of her family's analytical, emotional, and lighthearted characteristics. Chacha's family is hardy and upright, leaving painful emotions unspoken. In many senses, Chacha is the exception to his patriarchal family. His home was intergenerational, with his brothers' families living in the same compound. Chacha respected his brothers' wives for their quiet forbearance, and his mother for her capabilities as a single mother.

But still they both have difficulty adjusting to married life. Chacha struggles with his role as man of the house with a wife who was raised in a household where the woman was the breadwinner. Raani always wants to discuss relationship issues; Chacha would rather let them lie. America is demanding and lonely and it takes them time to reestablish their partnership.

When she finally meets Chacha's family in Pakistan a few years later, she swallows her anger at their rejection. They treat Chacha normally, but Raani does her best to charm them and fit in, especially by spinning stories for the children. Slowly, Raani grows to become an essential part of Chacha's family.

By their middle age, Chacha and Raani have become specialists in surgery and immunology, respectively, and leaders in the Muslim, Pakistani American, and medical communities. They have three overanalytical children—two girls early on, and then, after a period of eight years, a boy. Chacha and Raani do not teach their children to expect arranged marriage. There is an expectation that their children will marry Muslims, though not necessarily Pakistanis.

Raani's allergy practice allows her to come home early. She prepares the delicacies of her childhood—rice cooked in lamb broth, delicate kabobs, and eggplant in yogurt—as well as Chacha's favorite, *daal* and rice. The children yearn to spend more time with Chacha, who leaves for surgery before they wake up and comes home exhausted, sometimes spending entire Saturdays catching up on sleep. The children pursue careers in service, human rights, and academics. Raani and Chacha are disappointed, but have a hard time arguing against their passions.

Finally, the children leave for work or school. Chacha and Raani argue a little less and talk a little more. Their time is spent working toward a lifetime goal—building a *masjid* for their once-small midwestern Muslim community. Things are good.

They have two years of this.

Then, Raani is diagnosed with cancer. Her body reacts poorly to her treatment. She battles with illness over two grueling years, and dies in her home in the presence of Chacha, two of his siblings, four of her siblings, all three of her children, and a few cousins. It is the day of their wedding anniversary, and loyal Chacha left work before noon to bring home flowers, as he has done every year for over a quarter-century.

I, her youngest, was twenty-two years old.

II. A Set of Photos

I know Raani and Chacha's story because Ammi told me herself. As the oldest of six and a voracious reader, she found that telling stories was the best form of entertainment for the young ones. They gathered around her, listening to Api's grand tales with rapt attention. She later gave my sisters and me a romantic, detailed account of her life.

I have always struggled to understand what my father was like before he married Ammi. Like many men of his generation, Abu categorically refuses to speak about himself. My mother, ever the storyteller, provided much of the perspective we had on our father. As a child of a diplomat, he lived in Sudan, Saudi Arabia, and Pakistan. At fifteen, he lost his father. At eighteen, he hitchhiked alone through Kabul, Tehran, and Istanbul. The next year, he was in medical school. By twenty-five, he was married to my mother. When we asked him what his thought process was during these events, he said he couldn't remember.

During my teens, I wanted to grow up to be my mother. I found my father difficult. He had a temper and we argued often. I wanted to have the kind of analytical conversations I had with my mother, but he was either too tired from work or would tell me to ask Ammi. I sometimes questioned why someone like my mother would choose someone like my father.

With my mother gone, I see her choice more clearly. I see a man who is consistent and loyal. A man who is generous, with no sense of ego. A man who simply loves, because he has been showered with it his entire life. I have begun to see myself in him. I spent so much time empathizing with the pain my mother felt at being rejected by my father's family that I forgot to admire the deep love and courage my father demonstrated in marrying her.

With this in mind, I scramble through old albums at home to find the one photo we have of Ammi and Abu before they married. When I find it, I lie belly-down across my parents' bed and place the grayscale Polaroid in front of me.

The photo feels new to me. Chacha wears a crisp white shirt, black trousers, and thick, black frames. He appears the broad-shouldered son of Punjabi mustard fields that he is. Raani sits in the seat adjacent to Chacha in a sari, laughing. Her features bear the imprints of hilly Central Asia.

I turn to another photo. My father, in suit and tie, and my mother, in *lenhga*, both draped in garlands on their wedding. Chacha is smiling, eyes pinched. As a boy, I was told I was a replica of my mother. As a man, I do not see how my father's smile could be anything but mine.

My sisters and I always had a disconnect from Abu and struggled to understand him. He is by-the-rules. He avoids conflict. He honors the traditional relationship between younger and older siblings. Yet, he did this radically new thing: he married a working woman from a different caste. He had a love marriage. Is he not also, then, an extraordinary man?

The two Polaroids in front of me, I wonder what my father was thinking. I've never looked at these photos and thought of anyone but my mother. I notice something new: Abu is smiling ear to ear. My sisters and I used to laugh that he never learned how to fake a smile for pictures. But on his wedding day, he must have been incredibly happy. His radiant grin is a sign of their premarital love.

I look in his face, and I see mine. I look at Ammi and her face is a cipher. I can no longer know what this moment meant for her, the way I think about what it meant for Abu. I stare into Abu's face with a greater understanding of what came afterward.

III. A Question

I am twenty-five now, the age at which my parents married. Ammi has been gone for three years and I have done much to deal with the loss. Writing has been one manner of coping. Traveling, another. Relearning Urdu, the language my mother loved, a third. But my main way has been getting to know my father. In these three years, he has become my friend and my model for what it means to be a good human being. Still, I struggle to understand his choices.

One day, Abu speaks on the phone with one of his brothers. He offers advice on the school his brothers are building in Pakistan, giving his perspective in respectful tones. It's hard to imagine him as the rebel in his family. Later, I say:

"I've only seen you be a loving, supportive younger brother and son. So why did you disobey them on the most important thing—marriage?"

He says he does not know. Except that no one could point to the Qur'an and sunnah, and say, "Here. *This* is why you cannot marry a fellow Muslim woman."

I cannot get much more out of him. For most of his life, he relied on his wife to narrate, make meaning, and tell stories. He has come a long way in expressing himself since Ammi died, but much has been lost. I want to know about him. About Ammi.

IV. An Experiment

In my teenage and college years, I tried dating. I did my best to impart Islamic ethics onto my relationships, but, still, I felt guilty. I debated whether dating was inherently wrong and if it was my only option. I felt terrible about having to lie to my parents. Despite their history, they didn't have the language to speak about young love. When I finally told Ammi, the conversation was stilted and difficult. My mother teased me. Despite her insistence to the contrary, she told my father about what I had said. He acted like he never heard anything from her.

I knew that when it came time to marry, I would talk to Ammi, who would explain everything to Abu. With her gone, I do not know how this process works.

Initially, I didn't pursue Muslims. This was not because, as Ammi told me, "Muslims don't date." I never thought Muslim women would like me, with my long hair, ratty punk-rock T-shirts, and anti-capitalist rants. I went through my teens without one Muslim love interest.

As I grew older, I realized there were plenty of Muslims who did date. All those Muslims who didn't have arranged marriages met one another *somehow*. My parents never suggested that they would find someone for my sisters or me, so we searched in the only way that was available to us. I dated because I had no idea what other options I had.

When Ammi heard about my first relationship, I was told in calm tones that I would have to break up and that "good Muslim boys don't kiss girls." She was wearing her navy polka-dotted *shalwar kameez*, her *mehndi*-dyed hair not yet lost to chemotherapy. I had expected an argument, but discussions about relationships between us were calm. I think she was happy that I was interested in women. We had often butted heads over my long hair; she insisted it meant that I was gay, and I told her that was ridiculous and offensive.

In college, I grew a beard, cut my hair short and took punk rock off my T-shirts and left it in my headphones. Freshman year, I pursued medicine. My parents' community organizing stemmed in part from the status and security the medical profession affords. But my own mother had wanted to be a journalist or activist, involved in the worlds of public thought and justice, but had acquiesced to her father's wishes.

By sophomore year, I had dropped medicine for Islamic studies. As I learned about my cultural and religious inheritance, I realized I needed someone who shared the same values of feminism, justice, and diversity that my sisters, mother, and father raised me with. In my mother's view, Islam was something that endorsed all of these ideals.

That year, she became sick.

I transferred universities to help care for her. I had always made friends easily, but now, every time I met a new person, I suffered anxiety over what I could not share: *the most important person in my life is dying and I am a prisoner to that fact.* Often, I didn't talk about myself.

With Noor, it was easy.

The first time we spoke, we stood in the center of campus talking for two hours, paying no heed to the biting Michigan winter. She was close with someone I went to high school with, and we had just realized we had taken an entire semester of Urdu together. She was the first person I met after Ammi's diagnosis whom I felt comfortable with. Her own story involved parents of different backgrounds, but rather than coming from different castes, they came from different nations. Like Ammi with Abu, she regarded me with skepticism at first, thinking me underwhelming. Still, I noticed that, despite being a busy campus leader, she always took my phone calls.

One night a semester later, I decided to go on a bike ride. It was midnight and I was upset and lonely. I had mentioned the idea offhand to Noor earlier, so despite wanting to be alone, I messaged her. She joined me.

We biked to the edge of Ann Arbor and discussed our childhoods. I realized her value system was deeply similar to mine. I thought, *This is a strong, driven woman who wants to make a change in the world. She could be family.* I had just gotten out of a bad relationship, so there was no need to rush anything. I would be happy to have her in my life. Over the next two years, she became my best friend.

I don't know how, but eventually, she became something more. In the two of us I see a mixture of my father and mother. I have my mother's analytical mind and my father's straightforwardness; she has my mother's fearlessness in public spaces and my father's work ethic.

While my father accepted her immediately, I long for my mother's finicky protectiveness. I think my mother would have approved of her, but not before making her go through the most strenuous of tests. I know Abu will treat her with the same steadfastness and unequivocal love that he gives everyone in his life. Yet, something will always be missing. I struggle with the idea that my life partner will never have met my mother.

I spent all of this time trying to imagine my parents' early relationship so that it might inform my future. But subconsciously, I gained more than I realized from my parents' example. If you ask me why I chose who I did, my answer would be the same one Ammi gave me about why she married Abu.

She is my partner.

Sirat: The Journey

The Other Iran–Iraq War

By Ibrahim Al-Marashi

It was the Sunday before the start of my final year at UCLA. My parents had just driven me and a minivan loaded with my stuff from my hometown, Monterey, California, to the apartment I was sharing with friends. My parents were never the type to drop me off at school with a hug by the car and a wave from the window. My parents had to settle me in, a process that consisted of meeting my roommates, seeing my place, using the bathroom, saying their afternoon prayers, and making themselves a cup of tea.

The tea would usually lead to a trip to the grocery store. My father would rummage around in my cupboards looking for tea and sugar. Finding them bare, he would call out to my mother, who would declare my living arrangements unacceptable. No fruit. No bread. No sugar. No tea. No, son.

For my mother, leaving me in an apartment with bare cupboards was the same as leaving me in the desert with no water. She feared for my very survival. We would climb back into our Toyota minivan and head to their favorite grocery store in the neighborhood adjacent to UCLA, known as "Little Tehran," or "Tehrangeles." It was an Iranian grocery store, and my parents loved it. The store carried all the specialty foods they could not find in Monterey. They moved through the aisles, grabbing enough crisp thin cucumbers, leafy greens, firm eggplants, cookies, fruit leathers, pistachios, watermelon seeds, flat bread, and braided cheeses to last me an entire semester.

My father would take a grocery cart and make a dash for the produce. My mother would take her cart and head straight for the Persian pastries. I would make myself look busy with the newspapers and books arranged by the door, hoping I would not see anyone I knew.

But that day, I found myself drawn inside. I noticed an olive-skinned Iranian girl scanning the price of some fresh olives behind the checkout counter. It was around seven thirty in the evening, and the setting sun cast a golden glow on her skin and picked up the flecks of gold in her eyes. Her face was radiant. Engrossed in her work at the counter, she did not notice me staring at her. I made my way into the store, watching the way the sunlight danced across her auburn hair.

My eyes did not move from her face until I felt a small tap on my shoulder. "Quit looking at that girl. I am buying you all this food. The least you can do is help me."

At the sound of my mother's voice, the checkout girl looked up to find me blushing, my face redder than the pomegranates she sold to her customers.

My mom started to place the groceries onto the counter in her aisle and told me to finish while she pried my dad away from the produce section. After my mom left, the girl spoke, though the only word I could make out was *khoobi*?

"I'm sorry, but I don't speak Persian," I said, dumbfounded.

"You don't speak Persian? I can't believe you Persians who grow up in LA. You forget your language. Your culture." She shook her head disapprovingly. I was about to tell her that my parents were not Iranians but Arabs, Iraqis. But I couldn't find the words to say anything. Maybe she'd be offended that my family came from the country that waged war on hers. I just nodded and smiled, becoming the idiot I felt like I was.

My mom returned with my father, and I picked up the grocery bags with what dignity I had left and departed with my parents. They helped me take the groceries into my apartment and met my roommates, who had turned into perfect gentlemen. They moved their clothes off the sofa so my parents could sit down, and then pulled up chairs in front of them and made polite conversation in Arabic. But as soon as my parents left, they returned to being their regular uncouth selves. Clothes were piled back on the sofa, and the polite conversation turned to crude descriptions of the latest hot-girl sighting. I did not bring up the Iranian checkout girl. She was too special to mention in the raucous company of other guys—guys who would suddenly find reason to frequent the grocery store.

Our apartment was that cultural universal, the bachelor pad. Girly magazines covered our dining table, the sink was filled with unwashed dishes, and our stained blue-shag carpet had not been vacuumed since the day they moved in three months before me to attend the summer school session. The only furniture we had was a blue sofa we picked up off the sidewalk. We spent our evenings there, on its deflated cushions, watching whatever happened to be on TV.

Fadi and Samir were Palestinians who had been living in Kuwait until they were driven out by the 1991 Gulf War. I met them in 1993, just two years after they moved to the U.S., which meant they were both, for lack of a better term, F.O.B.s: "Fresh off the Boat." There was no greater proof of this than Fadi's fashion sense. His favorite T-shirt featured the words "Nice Vacation" on the front. Not "Have a Nice Vacation" or "I Had a Nice Vacation in California," but simply "Nice Vacation," with a little palm tree sticking out of the sand. His other favorite shirt had the periodic table of elements on it. That made Fadi a nerdy F.O.B.

In addition to the Palestinians, we had an Afghan roommate, Akbar, which made for an explosive mixture of Middle Eastern testosterone in one apartment. The others in our complex jokingly referred to our residence as "the refugee camp." Indeed, we sometimes embodied the volatile nature of Middle Eastern politics, forming shifting alliances against one another. The two of us who finally scraped all the hair out of the shower or washed the moldy mountain of dishes piled up in the sink would unite against the other two who stood by and watched. The alliances were temporary, and

I would be best friends with one of the Palestinians one day, only to form an Afghan–Iraqi axis the next day in an argument with the United Palestinian Bloc.

The morning after first seeing the Iranian checkout girl, I awoke feeling very scholarly. I scanned the course catalogue, looking for another class to add on to my schedule. But what would I take? How about Introduction to Persian? I looked up the times it was offered. I would have to wake up at the inhumane hour of 9 a.m. three times a week. It was a lot to consider.

I tried to legitimize my actions to myself. After eight years of war with Iran, it was high time an Iraqi made the effort to learn the Persian language. Perhaps taking Persian would be inconvenient, but it might just help smooth ties between Iraqis and Iranians the world over. Besides, if I were to run into the checkout girl, and she were to hear my smooth Persian, fall in love, and soon after marry me, wouldn't that be the greatest gift of all for our two cultures? Our children just might be the beginning of a beautiful Perso–Arab subculture.

I arrived for my first Persian class at 8:55 a.m. the following Wednesday. I was the only person there. By 9:05, the teacher, Miss Haqiqi, or Khanom Haqiqi, as she insisted we call her, showed up. At 9:10 the other students slowly filed into the classroom. More students arrived by 9:20, unusually late for a university class. While the class was at 9 a.m. according to the UCLA schedule, in reality it started according to Persian standard time, which meant somewhere between 9:15 and 9:20. By 9:30 there were sixty Iranian students and five "foreigners," as they called us non-Iranians, in the class.

On the first day, we learned how to say "*salaam*" (hello) and "*hal-e shoma chetawr ast?*" (How are you?). I repeated to myself over and over again, "*Salaam*, checkout girl, *hal-e shoma chetawr ast?*" With those few words, the class ended. I could not wait to visit her again. It had been a whole three days since I'd seen her.

I rode my bicycle to Tehrangeles, weaving in and out of the entourage of Persians driving black BMWs and Mercedes. My bike was also painted black, but somehow lacked the allure of the German sedans surrounding me. I parked a block away from the market, so the checkout girl would not see my pathetic efforts to tie my bike up to a parking meter. I even bought a BMW key chain to convince her that I owned a luxurious sports car.

I entered the store and avoided looking directly at her. I wanted to appear the food connoisseur, so I went straight for a metal basket and headed to the back of the store. After spending fifteen minutes gathering some groceries, I reached the counter and realized she was not there. I was tempted to put everything back, but I felt the eyes of the owner, a balding Iranian man, on me. He was probably the girl's father—my future father-in-law. I couldn't make a bad impression. So I paid for an assortment of things I had no need for: spices, dried limes, sour cherries, and a few tomatoes. I returned for her on Thursday, Friday, and Saturday. She failed to show, but her father continued to give me curious glances, no doubt confused by the odd combination of items I chose.

Sunday came and I was confident that since she had not been in all week, she would be there that morning. I showered, shaved, and put on my best clothes, a white long-sleeve shirt stained under the arms, a pair of black slacks that were a bit short on me, and chunky black loafers that I wore with the only socks I owned, white gym socks. Besides those few items, my wardrobe consisted of various white T-shirts, shorts, and a pair of sandals.

I rode my bike to the market, parked it at the same parking meter a block away, and entered the store, looking directly at the counter. After a week, I was finally reunited with the checkout girl. I realized that she must work only on Sundays, the day when her father's store was the busiest. She was such a loyal daughter that I felt sad for a moment at the thought that I would one day sweep her away, leaving him to face his Sunday shoppers alone.

I grabbed a metal basket, but it stuck to the others and I knocked the entire stack down. She looked in my direction and shook her head disapprovingly. I was off to a bad start. I began placing groceries in my basket, grabbing items off the shelf, sending quick glances at her while walking between the aisles. After spending nearly forty-five minutes "shopping," I approached the counter. My metal basket shook after I noticed her father standing by the fruit section, eyeing me suspiciously.

I placed the items one by one on the counter and said triumphantly to her, "*Salaam. Hal-e shoma chetwar ast?*"

She replied with several words I couldn't understand.

She waited for an answer, sighed under her breath, and shook her head again disapprovingly. Heartbroken, I took my grocery bags and left.

Another week passed and I studied so diligently for my Persian class that I neglected my other courses. I was intimidated by the other students in the class, Iranian boys and girls dressed in the latest Gucci and Armani fashions, always in black. Even at 9:30 a.m. they looked ready for a night on the town, while I looked ready to wash cars.

I was also intimidated by their language skills. Most spoke Persian at home and were taking the class for an easy "A," to boost their grade point average so that they could get into the prestigious law or medical school of their parents' choice. In that respect I did not envy them. My parents had the same wishes for me, but I had chosen to ignore their dreams and study Middle Eastern history. Most of my classmates still hoped to become members of one of the few professions esteemed among Middle Easterners: medicine, engineering, or law, to the neglect of the humanities and arts.

I always sat next to an Iranian American student named Maziar, who was different from the Tehrangeles types. He wore jeans and a simple short-sleeve shirt. His mother was white and since he'd learned only the basics of Persian growing up, he was taking the class to actually learn the language. Unlike the other students, he made an effort to talk to me. He was curious about a "foreigner" trying to learn Persian. He had resisted his father's pressure to study medicine and was studying film instead.

Maziar was cynical about the other Iranian students, and he nicknamed our class the "kebab meat market." After seeing a boy flirt with a girl, he shook his head and said, "I don't even know why he bothers. Persian guys can only propose to the families of Persian girls when they have their law or medical degree, car, and house. By the time this guy has all those things, he's going to be fatter and balder and looking for a younger woman. You'll see. He's not going to get married for at least another six to ten years. His future wife is not in this classroom. She's just barely starting middle school."

Visiting the checkout girl on Sunday mornings became a weekly ritual. On Saturday nights while my roommates were out clubbing, I stayed home to rehearse Persian dialogues. On Sunday morning, when they were sleeping in, I was waking up, shaving, showering, and making my pilgrimage to the market.

During one trip, I noticed she wore a Salvador Dali shirt, and it struck me how different she was from the other Iranian girls in my class, who were so preoccupied with their clothes and makeup. She wore no makeup and a simple T-shirt, and yet she was so beautiful. She did not notice me enter, and I brought my groceries up to her, ready to ask her out to a museum. Just as I was about to open my mouth, her father came and stood at her side. I bought the groceries without saying anything and headed out the door.

As I was leaving, a white friend of mine walking on the street passed by and saw me through the store window. He entered and smiled at her, checking out my checkout girl. He pulled me aside and said, "Is she Mexican?"

I pushed him out of the store, since he was far better looking than me, but he kept on insisting on going back inside.

"Is she Latina?"

"No, she is Persian."

"Damn, I have to go to Persia."

"No, I mean she is Iranian."

"I-ranian? She ain't no daughter of the Ayatollah!"

The next day, I sat in class dreaming about my checkout girl when Khanom Haqiqi demanded in her elongated English, "Ibrahim, read what is on the board!" The Persian alphabet was in itself an art form. A subtle dot or a line could change the entire meaning of a word. I learned that lesson the hard way that day.

"*K . . . ki . . . kiiir . . . kir.*" All the Iranian students in the class burst into laughter.

"Ibrahim, *kir nagu, gir bagu!*" In other words, "Don't say '*kir*,' say '*gir*.'"

I had just read what I thought I saw on the board. I asked Maziar, "Why is everyone laughing at me?" He told me that instead of saying what the teacher had written on the board, the word "obtain," I had said, "Penis." The difference between "*kir*" and "*gir*" was one slanted line that I had failed to see.

In spite of being painfully embarrassed, I wasn't discouraged. On that day, not only did I learn the Persian word for a male body part, but I learned the phrase, "*Qorban-e shoma,*" which literally means, "I sacrifice myself for you." It was simply a way of saying thank you. That phrase described my feelings for the checkout girl. I sacrificed my time and effort to learn her language, as well as my pride and dignity in her presence. For those few moments at the counter in the grocery store, I could honestly say to her, "*Qorban-e shoma.*"

Over the course of the semester, I was able to converse with her in Persian. My greatest triumph was the small smile she gave me one afternoon when she noted the progress I was making. I had won her approval, and that moment of sweet reward was enough to bring me back to her counter week after week.

One Saturday night, I decided that I had to tell her how I felt. I would do it early the next day. By then, I had garnered that my future father-in-law liked sleeping in on Sundays and generally walked in an hour after the store opened. I had convinced myself it was divine intervention that arranged our meeting. God's plan began when my parents left Iraq in the sixties. What if my parents had stayed in Iraq? I could have been one of "them." Picked up off the streets of Baghdad during the Iran–Iraq War and dispatched to the front lines. It could have been my hands that killed one of her relatives or my eyes that watched one of her family members get eaten alive by the corrosive chemical agents the Iraqi military used during the eight-year conflict. Or I could have ended up as a number, a casualty of battle, like the thousands of other young Iraqi men I had read about. What if the checkout girl's parents had stayed in Iran? She might have read about my death among the Iraqi casualties and said, "Good. Those Iraqis deserve to die for attacking our land." Instead, we were both the products of exile. And, thanks to our parents, we could look at each other across a checkout counter, instead of a militarized international border.

On that Saturday night, Samir, one of my Palestinian roommates, stormed in wearing his nightclub uniform, a black shirt unbuttoned down to his belly button with his Black Forest of chest hairs on display for the world and tight black jeans, awash in sweat and cheap cologne. He was so upset that I knew something serious had happened.

He threw himself on the sofa and sighed, "Yeah, so I saw this girl dancing and walked up to her and grabbed her. And you know, started to do the 'grind' with her." He jumped up onto the couch and gyrated his pelvis into her imaginary body and then plopped himself back down. "And she pushed me away. And I was thinking, 'What's wrong with the beeetch?' I see the guys. They do it all the time with girls on MTV."

"But those guys on MTV are rappers, and they have a lot of money. They can get away with a lot of things you can't," I answered. Of all of us in the apartment, I was the only one who was American born, which carried a certain weight of responsibility. It was my duty to properly socialize my immigrant friends.

I was not alone in this project. Being an Iraqi American meant that I could count myself among the other Arab American students. As a group we had a ranking system for those Arab students who had just arrived from the Middle East to study at UCLA, and the level of acculturation they would subsequently require. *F.O.B.* referred to anyone with a heavy Arab accent who tried so hard to fit in with the American lifestyle that he wound up standing out. For example, Arabs in cowboy hats, Arabs who misused slang terms, Arabs who watched the Super Bowl. An *F.O.C.* was "Fresh Off the Camel," which we used only to refer to those students from Saudi Arabia (even we Arabs discriminate among ourselves). And *S.O.B.* stood for "Still on Board," or, in other words, a student who did not realize he had left the Middle East and dressed like he was walking on the streets of Cairo. My Palestinian roommate was somewhere in between an F.O.B. and an S.O.B.—the latter in the original sense of the abbreviation.

He continued, "Whatever. Then I went up to another girl and told her, 'You must dance with me.' She said, 'No. Get out of here, you creep.' I told her, 'You will dance with me. It will be berfect.'" Grinding his teeth and clenching his fists, he whined, "Ibrahiiiim, I need a blonde girl soooo badly. They turn me on soooo much."

The following day, I rode my bike into Tehrangeles and parked it once again a block away. The checkout girl had a cold that day. Although her nose was red from blowing into tissues, she still looked beautiful to me. I filled my basket until it overflowed, too nervous to approach. When the customer she was helping finally walked away, I approached her register and tried to muster enough courage to express my feelings.

Just as she finished ringing up the last pomegranate, her father entered the store. He said good morning to her in Persian and then kissed her on her lips. I thought I was going to throw up. What kind of disgusting incest had I just witnessed? Then I noticed it—a thin gold wedding band on her finger. How had I never seen it before? I felt the heat rushing to my cheeks like it did when I'd been caught staring at her by my mom. And, just like on that day, my face turned redder than a pomegranate. All that time, energy, and money spent over the last three months. All those Persian lessons, groceries, and poetry—and she was married. It was fortunate that I did not confess my feelings for her while her husband was around. It would have led to an Iran–Iraq War in the grocery store, with pomegranates thrown instead of grenades.

In my obsession with the checkout girl, I had failed to appreciate that I had entered a new world and experienced a new culture. During those language courses, I was introduced to Iranian history, architecture, literature, cinema, and poetry. Even though I was studying Persian for the sake of the checkout girl, I was falling in love with the language and culture. The already lamentable war between Iraq and Iran had become a tangible tragedy to me.

I took my groceries for the last time and left the store without a single word. I gave the food to the first homeless man I saw and walked home, forgetting about my bike. On my way back, I realized that although I had made all that effort for that girl, I never knew her name. In my mind, I called her Scheherazade. While she did not entertain me with 1,001 tales, my quest for her gave me my own tale.

Just One Kiss

By Maher Reham

I could feel her bare breasts rubbing against my chest.

I could taste her menthol lip balm when we kissed. She could never get the taste of double-apple hookah off her tongue.

She was conscious of her crooked teeth, but I loved her smile. Women don't understand that their imperfections make them unique.

I ran my hands down her back. So many times I'd fantasized about her at the office. She was a *hijabi* and had seemed so religious. I'm a practicing Muslim, too. But here we were.

Even then my excitement was tainted by sharp pangs of guilt.

I wish I could say that it hurt whenever I thought about Allah and the *haram* we were doing. But that wasn't it. I knew Allah was forgiving—that helped me justify it. But there was one person who wasn't forgiving.

My wife.

How the hell did I get here?

As I write this, the pain, chaos, and euphoria of two years ago are all coming back. I often wonder why I cheated on my wife. Growing up, I was praised for my good character. My mother's friends adored me and wanted their daughters to marry me. The youth of the community wanted to be like me. Fathers respected me and asked me to counsel their sons.

Would they still if they knew?

Infidelity is an epidemic in American society; the Muslim community is no exception. The practicing Muslim brothers I grew up with were involved in *masjid* youth activities and loathed anything immoral. Now, in our mid-thirties, 90 percent of my group has had an emotional or physical extramarital affair. Perhaps some of that can be traced to the fact that many of our fathers (including mine) had secret second wives.

I'm not perfect. No one is.

My parents are active, religious pillars of their community. They met in their hometown, Kuala Lumpur, married, and moved to New York to study. That's where I was born and raised, among immigrants who brought their extremely conservative, cultural understandings of Islam with them. They were terrified of their children becoming "American," particularly given the country's loose views on sex. If as a youth you were caught talking to a girl, it was tantamount to having premarital sex.

While I had strong sexual urges, I adhered to my community's beliefs. But I struggled. As early as third grade, my classmates had boyfriends and girlfriends. By high school, my strength to hold back was waning. I didn't proactively seek a girlfriend, but it was hard watching everyone else around me partake, including Muslim peers.

I remained committed to never having a girlfriend or committing *zina*, but I couldn't contain my sexual urges. I discovered masturbation and porn. You might say a Muslim teen believing that *zina* is *haram* while simultaneously being obsessed with porn is a contradiction, but I didn't know what else to do with my natural urges. I figured porn was the lesser of two evils, but I still had tremendous guilt.

Scarlett caught my eye my first week at Brooklyn College. I had a thing for blondes and she seemed to be the "it girl" on campus. Months later, I heard that she was planning on converting to Islam at the Muslim Students' Association (MSA) Ramadan banquet.

That night, she uttered the *shahada* onstage. The crowd cheered. Sisters hugged her, brothers—including me—congratulated her. Over the next couple of months, the MSA kids became her new family. I was the MSA treasurer, but it wasn't until a bunch of us decided to take a road trip to see Dave Chappelle that we connected. She was beautiful, sweet, genuine. She and I participated in group conversations, where I found out about her interests in music, poetry, anthropology, and stand-up.

Over the next couple of months, Scarlett and I became closer. But I didn't know how to pass the friend zone. I'd spent my life avoiding girls; this was uncharted territory. We gave each other sweet gifts, and had long conversations over the phone, sometimes till the early morning hours. But I was too shy to say anything, too afraid of rejection. I just hoped Allah would provide me an opening if a relationship with her was right for me.

Toward the end of the semester, I poured out my feelings about Scarlett to our mutual friend Asma.

"*SubhanAllah.* Last night, Scarlett told me she's in love with you!" Asma exclaimed.

I waited a week before I did anything with this information.

I decided to pass Scarlett a note. "I have something to tell you. Let's meet at the water fountain in the middle of campus?"

That night I said, "Scarlett, I love your personality, I think you have a clean and genuine heart. I think you'd make a great mother and a great wife. You're beautiful inside and out and my feelings for you have grown to more than friendship. I think you feel the same way. Am I right?"

It made my heart melt when she bit her lip, tried to control her smile, and nodded. I could see the tears of happiness well up in her eyes.

I couldn't hug her. I didn't have a ring. I didn't have the money to marry her. I was in my second year of college. So what now?

We talked all night. Our plan was to wait. Two more years to graduation, and then I'd find a job. No touching until then.

✧   ✧   ✧

As we got to know each other better, however, it became clear that we weren't completely compatible. I was a relaxed slacker; she was anal and organized. I was just getting by academically; she was a straight-A student. She loved anthropology; I was into engineering. I loved hip-hop and spoken word; she loved alternative music and heavy metal.

Because of my inexperience with women, I was insecure. I'd be furious when I saw her having coffee with or learning guitar from a male friend and would accuse her of flirting.

We began to fight. I remember us yelling and cussing in the library. At the park. In the cafeteria. It became more frequent until we were arguing every day.

The bad times were bad, but the good times were really good, so, despite all the fighting, we never wanted to let go.

We'd been together a year and hadn't yet touched. I still had a year to graduation and then had to convince my parents to let me marry a convert, so there was no light at the end of the tunnel.

One day, a group of us were at her apartment watching a movie. Our hands rested lightly on the armrest between us. Her hand barely caressed mine. That's as far as we could go in a roomful of MSAers.

As soon as the door closed behind them, we hugged for the first time. Finally. It felt so good.

I kissed her forehead. Then, her cheek.

Before I knew it, we were making out, ferociously kissing, gasping for air. My hands were roaming her body. She put her hands between my legs as I pulled up her shirt and pulled off her bra.

SLAM!

Her roommate's door flung open and we could hear footsteps coming our way. We frantically put our clothes back on.

"Hey, guys," said Ruby politely.

"Hey," I said.

We sat awkwardly as Ruby grabbed a glass of water and returned to her room.

"Do you think she noticed?" I whispered.

"Ummm, I'm not wearing my *hijab* . . ."

Over the next couple of weeks, we had many physical encounters, including oral sex, but never went all the way. We knew we were approaching *zina*. After much thought and discussion, we anonymously e-mailed some imams whose opinions we trusted. They agreed with our decision: a secret marriage is better than *zina*.

In a ceremony at Asma's house, we eloped for a dowry of $4.

That night, we rented a hotel room with a Jacuzzi.

We prayed two *rakat*. I opened the Qur'an and, like a miracle, it opened to the *ayah* forbidding *zina*. We had made the right decision.

I lost my virginity that night. I'd waited twenty years for this. It's all I wanted to do for the rest of the weekend. But the few times I approached Scarlett, she stopped me: "Let's not get carried away. Let's do other things, too." I felt embarrassed and rejected.

We had sex several times that weekend. But it was uncomfortable. Like we didn't fit.

We were married in secret for a year. Publicly we were engaged; privately we met at hotels to have sex.

Eventually, after convincing our parents, we had a small official wedding. It felt good to be able to finally walk down the street and not worry about anyone seeing us. We found a studio in the cheap part of town, excited to start our lives together.

The first night there, we were sitting on our cheap Craigslist couches. I put my arms around her and my hands in her pants.

"HEY!" She jerked away, screaming frantically. "Excuse me! What are you doing?!"

"What? Nothing . . . I guess." I felt embarrassed and stupid. For the last decade of my life, I'd been waiting to have sex. I'd hardly talked to girls and had a fear of rejection, and here I was being rejected by my own wife. It was the ultimate humiliation.

Scarlett and I loved each other. We talked intimately about our feelings, but her bad experiences with sex before she became Muslim warped her thinking. She was uncomfortable and, in turn, made me uncomfortable. Added to our other incompatibilities, this drove the wedge deeper between us.

Married life was nothing like I thought it would be. What happened to the sex-crazed college kids? We rarely had sex. I reverted to masturbation. I lashed out, belittling her so she'd feel as small as I did after she rejected me.

She lost a drastic amount of weight. She became a slob, clothes and dishes everywhere. I was home most of the time, making my own meals and paying the bills. She went out with her friends, spending thousands of dollars each month on herself. This fed our shouting matches.

We loved each other, but we didn't like each other. I respected her passion. Her discipline. Her generosity. She was a good person. She knew I was doing everything I could to take care of her. We often said, "I love you, and I want to make this work." That we'd never found anyone else like each other. Despite the lack of sex, we showed affection through frequent kisses and hugs. But we couldn't be in a room together for more than a day without a world war breaking out.

For years, I kept thinking, "Is marriage supposed to be like this?" I sought advice from elders in the community, but no one gave me anything concrete. It was always, "Marriage is a struggle, gotta deal with it. It will get better." But when?

I felt a tremendous amount of injustice. What am I getting from this marriage? My sexual frustration coupled with my humiliation and failure as a man made me tense all the time.

The last straw came six years into our marriage when Scarlett said, "I bought a ticket to California with my friends for my birthday."

With no consideration, permission, or consultation, she bought the ticket. With my money. And, instead of spending her birthday with her husband, she preferred to spend it with her friends.

That's when I realized she had no respect for me.

I worked as a programmer at software companies. I loved poetry and performed at different Muslim conferences. I was getting play from lots of women—Muslim and non-Muslim.

But I had more honor than that. As unsatisfied as I was, I had made a vow. So I resisted their advances for years, coming home to a wife who withheld sex and cursed me out.

I got a programming job at Wells Fargo. They told me there was a Muslim banker there named Bushra. She was the wife of a prominent community member, but I'd never met her.

I was stunned when I did. "That chubby, old guy married . . . HER?" I thought. She was young, vibrant, and very attractive. Even though her teeth were a little crooked, she had a beautiful smile. She knew Scarlett from the *masjid*, as I knew her husband.

She didn't seem as conservative as I'd initially thought. She liked the same music as me, which was weird knowing how religious her husband was. She loved poetry and was impressed by mine. She laughed at my jokes. It felt good to be valued like that again.

Often, she'd come in to work flustered, almost in tears. I told myself it was my duty to make sure she was okay. We started chatting online. Eventually, she poured her heart out about her rocky marriage. I told her I understood and that she should end it if she didn't see a future, or try to save it if she did.

"But you and Scarlett seem so solid . . ." she typed. She was fishing for the real story. I gave it to her.

Over the next couple of months, Bushra and I comforted each other when our spouses weren't there for us. We gave each other marital advice. Her relationship was unsalvageable by the time we met. I was there to comfort her during her divorce.

My intentions were innocent. Though I was attracted to Bushra, I didn't want any complications. But I couldn't help but fantasize about her.

I could feel the same energy coming from Bushra that I had from Scarlett in the past. She acted like a conservative Muslima around everyone else, but around me, she was flirtatious. She liked me.

I could see things evolving to more than a friendship. This worried me. I realized that I needed to make sure that I didn't lose the woman I loved. Scarlett had started to work on gaining weight, which helped us sexually. I had trained myself not to want her because of her repeated rejections, but that night I forced myself to have sex.

A month later, she interrupted my closed-door poetry writing session.

"Oh my God! Babe, you're not going to believe this—I'm pregnant!"

We were stunned but hugged each other in happiness.

But I was also nervous. Was I ready to be a father? Were we ready?

Scarlett left for California for two weeks to spend her birthday with her girlfriends.

I was alone.

During those two weeks, Bushra was coy and flirty. I did my best not to participate, but it felt good to be desired.

One night online, I asked, "Why are you doing this?"

I could tell by her pause that she was taken by surprise. "Can't you just take this how it is?"

"Listen, it seems like you're attracted to me. I'm attracted to you too. But it can't go any further." There was a pause again. "Are you there?"

"I'm sorry. It won't happen again. I can't believe you feel this way about me. I thought it was one-sided. You don't know how much I needed to hear this in my life right now."

While ending things was the goal of my conversation, I couldn't deny the excitement I felt.

I picked up Scarlett that night, but I couldn't stop thinking about Bushra. The next day, true to her word, Bushra didn't speak to me.

We did our best to stay away from each other, but working together didn't help and, as time went on, we got to know each other intimately. She told me how her daddy issues made her search for love in the wrong places, leading to a promiscuous youth. Men always wanted her for her body, and left after they got that. She tried to turn her life around by marrying her husband, a conservative Muslim, but there had never been any sparks there. He couldn't satisfy her.

She fell for me because I was the only guy in her life who cared about her but didn't want to get in her pants.

Bushra and I chatted online nightly. Scarlett thought I was catching up on old episodes of *Lost*. But I had a secret life. Secret profiles, e-mails, codes, texts. Because of my paranoia, we were never even close to getting caught.

One day, Bushra pinged me on chat. "I had a dream about you last night. That you hugged me. It felt so amazing. I have something to ask you . . . could you come over to my apartment and give me a hug? Just one."

"I can't. I know myself. I'll want more."

"You're right. I'm sorry."

I felt bad. I wanted her to know that it wasn't because I didn't like her but because it wasn't the right thing to do.

She was persistent. Each day, she asked, and each day, I rejected her. After a week, I gave in. It was only a hug.

When I parked in her driveway, my heart was racing. The danger of getting caught aroused me.

She opened the door and we embraced. After a couple of minutes, I left.

Over the next couple of weeks, I visited Bushra's apartment before and after work. We hugged and talked, until one night she cried as I walked to her door to leave.

"I'm sorry. Things are hard for me right now. I feel so alone. And you make me feel good about myself again."

I wiped the tear from her eye and kissed her on the forehead. Then I kissed her on the lips. We looked each other in the eyes and then kissed for twenty minutes straight. I took off her headscarf and started kissing her neck.

We managed to pull away, and I left her apartment.

The avalanche of guilt almost suffocated me. I had crossed a line. Bushra now talked about sex all the time. We'd chat dirty at work and about our darkest fantasies on the phone. We'd sneak hugs at work, kisses in the break room, play footsie in meetings. I was never this open with Scarlett. I felt free.

We knew what we were doing was wrong. Several times we wrote each other good-bye letters, but then I'd be back at her apartment. Later, I'd kiss my pregnant wife while she slept.

Something had to give. Allah allows men to take another wife—this had to be the reason. I decided I was going to do this right. Things weren't working out with Scarlett and I was tired of being the scumbag. I was going to be honest. We were going to do this the halal way.

One day, I took Scarlett to the school across the street. "I have something to tell you."

"What is it? You're scaring me."

Neither of us could look the other in the eye. Maybe she knew what was coming. "Things aren't working out between us. I don't want to lose you and the baby. But my needs aren't being met. I want a second wife."

Tears started welling in Scarlett's eyes: "I hate you, motherfucker!"

She darted across the street but I caught her. We fought all the way back to the apartment.

She didn't come out of our bedroom that night. I texted her telling her we needed space, so I was going to my mother's house.

I got to Bushra's apartment as fast as I could, practically breaking down the door. That was the night she took off her shirt and I took off mine.

For the next year and through the birth of my daughter, Bushra and I became closer. She was fine with the idea of being one of two wives. Our plan was to wait till I could win Scarlett over.

Scarlett and I were at each other's throats, barely having sex, always fighting, and raising an infant at the same time. The wall was riddled with holes. Holes from my fists, holes from throwing the table at the wall, from throwing dishes. But the thought of losing everything I had built with someone I had loved for so many years hurt.

In a twisted way, I believed that marrying Bushra would allow me to keep Scarlett. Scarlett and I weren't connecting emotionally because I wasn't satisfied physically. It wasn't only physical with Bushra, but she could fulfill my sexual needs and reduce the tension in my first relationship. I thought being with them would make me a better husband to both.

Bushra comforted me, but hiding in the shadows took its toll. She started to threaten me with seeing other men.

I had to make a choice.

Ironically, on the anniversary of the night I had told Scarlett that I loved her, I sat her down again. "We've been trying, but it's not working. I'm sorry. Let me have a second wife, or I want a divorce."

Tears dripped down Scarlett's face. "Fine," she sobbed. She couldn't accept a second wife, so she agreed to a divorce.

I was sad, but relieved. This was going to hurt, but it was the right thing to do.

I called one of Scarlett's friends, Fatima, to our home to mediate my departure. Shortly after Fatima arrived, Scarlett said, "I have something to ask you."

After a moment of silence, I said, "Well? What?"

"Is anything going on between you and Bushra?"

How the hell did she know? We'd been so careful. But she knew me better than anyone else.

Ashamed, I looked down, slowly nodding yes.

To this day, I'm not sure what came first, the cry of agony or her fists. Before I knew it, I was being slapped from every angle. Punching, kicking, scratching. The emotional scars left from that fight still hurt.

Fatima jumped on Scarlett, trying to hold her back.

"I'M GOING TO KILL YOU! I'M GOING TO GET MY DAD TO KILL YOU!"

After a couple of minutes, she calmed down. I headed for the door. Scarlett grabbed my arms.

Within seconds, Scarlett had crumpled to the floor, sobbing uncontrollably. I had never seen her this broken. It hurt to know I had done that to her.

I told Fatima to leave. I picked Scarlett up and hugged her. "I'm sorry. You know I love you. I don't know where things went wrong. I've tried everything with you. For years. Counseling. 'Faking it till we make it.' I've resisted other girls for years. But you and I, it's just not . . . fitting. And this . . . just happened."

Scarlett tried to compose herself. She looked into my eyes and asked, "What happened to you and me? It was supposed to be you and me. Remember?"

That's when I lost it. This was the Scarlett I fell in love with—the sweet, kind girl who wanted nothing but to be with me.

"You're going to throw away what we have, what we built, for a girl you barely know?"

I hated myself for hurting both of these women. But I had to make a choice.

Should I pick the woman who seduced a married man? A woman who was struggling with her morality? A woman like me?

Or the woman whose morals I never questioned? A woman who stuck by me for years and who, in spite of the pain and what I did to her, still wanted to work it out? A woman better than me?

The next day, I didn't go to work. Bushra contacted me online. "Is everything okay?"

"Yah."

"You told her, didn't you."

"Yes."

"And?"

"Can we not talk about it like this?"

"Just say it. You chose her, didn't you?"

I paused. Then typed, "It's not going to work between you and me."

I could almost see the look on Bushra's face. The hurt. The self-pity.

She wrote, "See. I told you. They always leave. Even you."

That was the last time I talked to Bushra and my last day at Wells Fargo. Blocked on Facebook. Unfollowed on Twitter. Chats blocked. Secret e-mails closed. Poetry deleted.

I think about Bushra every day. The smell of double-apple tobacco reminds me of her. I think about the pain I caused her. I wonder if she thinks about me. I'll never forget her, and I'll always thank her for filling the cracks of my heart when I needed them to be filled.

But then I step back, and I look at my heart as a whole and I see Scarlett. She is my heart. I made the right decision. I don't ever want her to go through that pain again.

It scares me how close I got to leaving.

Things aren't perfect between Scarlett and me, but when we hit rock bottom we realized what we had to lose. We went to counseling, and that has helped. Every time one of us wants to fight for their rights or is upset at what our relationship is missing, we remember how close we came to losing each other, and all of a sudden, we forget what we're missing and realize what we have. Our life, sexually and emotionally, isn't perfect, but we try to meet in the middle.

Happy ending? In progress.

AwkwardMan

By Zain Omar

I often think awkwardness is my superpower. No one else I know has such a deft way of turning an ordinary situation into a hot mess of confusion and apprehension. People have noticed—particularly at work, where I seem to bumble my way through meetings and pleasantries with high-powered executives.

When I tell people I work in online marketing, I usually get a confused response: they assume that I work from home in a get-rich-quick scheme or that I'm spamming their e-mail address about performance-enhancing drugs. It's still a fairly new field, and it doesn't yet have much cachet because there hasn't been a television series to glamorize it.

In one of my many attempts to legitimize my life's work, I started a job in Los Angeles with the hopes of turning the phrase "I work in online marketing" into "I am an executive at a marketing firm." However, my inner AwkwardMan took over and sabotaged me before I could get a firm grip on the corporate ladder.

"That's a good-looking coffee cup," said the CEO of the company as I arrived last to my first significant meeting.

"Thanks!" I replied, excitedly. "I got it to match my good-looking face!"

As a deafening silence fell over the conference room full of important people, I realized that my humor did not translate well to this audience.

I like to think that AwkwardMan could be a new superhero—maybe not one invited to the same parties as Batman and Superman, but definitely part of the nerdy group that includes Quailman and

Captain Planet. I imagine that my superhero cape would be just a little too long and loose fitting, something that would get caught in a doorway as I made my triumphant entrance to catch the bad guys. Then, as I stumbled clear, it would rip in half. Not to be deterred, I'd attempt to halt them with a catchy and powerful tagline, but mispronounce a word or have trouble projecting the phrase loudly enough, and they'd stop briefly, struggling to understand what I'd said. "AwkwardMan Inconveniences Bad Guys!" would be my signature headline in the newspapers.

I wasn't always so uneasy in social settings. In fact, for most of my life I enjoyed meeting new people. I moved to the United States from England when I was fourteen and quickly found that having an English accent had many benefits—people seemed to like talking to me, regardless of what I was actually saying. It's much easier to start conversations with new people when you know that at some point they will use the phrase "I love your accent." That kind of instant validation made socializing less daunting to a natural introvert.

It was only during the last couple of years—after a hurtful breakup with a woman I nearly married—that I developed an intense unease. To say that my self-confidence was affected by the breakup would be an understatement. To this day, no words have taken as intense an emotional toll as when my then-fiancée said: "You are a horrible person, I hate you, and I hope you never hurt another girl the way that you hurt me."

That sentence reverberated in my heart, destroying my self-image. I had always imagined myself to be a kind person who went out of his way to help others. But if the person I nearly married could say that about me, maybe I didn't know who I was after all. Maybe I was a bad person. Maybe I was kidding myself that I could be in a healthy relationship, or even a friendship with anyone, because I would only end up hurting them. This internalization was the birth of AwkwardMan.

Confidence and self-esteem were aspects of my personality that I only fully appreciated when I could no longer feel them. I changed from a person comfortable talking to new people to one preoccupied with self-doubt in every interaction. At one social gathering a few months after the breakup, I was so nervous that I spilled my plate of food three times. My existing network of friends were close with both me and my ex-fiancée and, not wanting to cause any issues, I withdrew from that crowd, preferring the comfort of my own company rather than having to answer questions about what had happened between us.

As I withdrew from social circles, AwkwardMan flourished. Life became very lonely—although I did start a great friendship with my Roomba robot vacuum. He was a friendly little guy, working away on the carpet on Friday nights as I heated up frozen pizza and complained about what had happened at work that week. Roomba was a great listener.

My apartment slowly turned into its own fortress of solitude. Aside from work, I only ventured out to play in a local pickup soccer game on the weekends. I even renamed my Wi-Fi network Quantum of Solace as a passive plea in the hopes that my neighbors might want to hang out. They didn't.

When an old friend came into town and insisted we go out to eat so that I could meet his wife, I went out for the first time in months. It turned out to be an entertaining night, made easier by pleasant company and good food. I had awkward moments, but the conversation flowed well enough that they weren't too apparent.

However, the next day highlighted the extent of my isolation. My credit card company called me in the morning.

"Sir, we have some unusual activity on your card—can you verify these charges?" The caller then proceeded to list all of the previous night's charges.

"Yes, those are good. Anything else?" I replied.

"No, that was all the unusual activity we found. Thank you, your card's temporary suspension has been lifted."

I couldn't help but laugh after the call ended. I knew my credit card company's fraud monitoring system had a sophisticated algorithm to protect accounts. If I suddenly used my card in a new city they would call me. Or, if I made a huge purchase, I would get an alert. But this time, I triggered an alarm because the company calculated that based on my purchase habits, there was little likelihood that I would be out on a Friday evening, let alone getting sushi and crepes. By their logic, it had to have been someone else.

That was a turning point. I knew things had to change.

Reflecting on my postbreakup life, I realized I had actively isolated myself, punishing myself for everything that had happened in the relationship. While I was to blame for certain things, we shared responsibility for many of our problems. The hurt of my ex's last words still lingered, making me doubt that I deserved good things. However, after a year of nights at home with Roomba, and after my credit card company decided that going out on a Friday night was completely out of character, I realized I needed to start saying yes more often. I needed to relive those old days when I was genuinely excited by the company of others. I even resolved to exaggerate my English accent, if needed.

AwkwardMan didn't like this rejuvenated spirit. He struggled with and fought me at every step, whispering that I didn't deserve to have any fun or that I was a horrible person. At times, I listened and gave in, but mainly I pushed on, spurred by my new goal of spending one day per week in a social setting. I reconnected with old friends (who were happy to see me again), found groups of young Muslims to hang out with, and attended events where I managed not to make a fool of myself. Friday nights, once dedicated to video game marathons, might find me instead at a *Star Wars* concert at the Hollywood Bowl. I went from sleeping in on Saturday mornings until noon to driving to Orange County at 8 a.m. to volunteer at a food bank. Slowly, I rebuilt my social circle. It was difficult, and talking to new people still held some challenges, but it ended up being more worthwhile than I ever could have imagined.

Here's what happened: I was meeting a new friend, Muna, at the mall, where we were planning to catch a movie. Initially, I couldn't find Muna in the crowd. When I finally did, I joked that her new workout routine was so effective that when she turned sideways she disappeared. Don't worry, she didn't laugh either. Another victory for AwkwardMan!

Muna let it pass and brought me over to say a quick hello to a group of her friends that I hadn't met before. Like every great comedian, I used the same material again on these young ladies, thinking my obvious charm and good looks would carry the joke successfully this time. They did not.

As yet another awkward silence lingered in the air, my winning smile deteriorated from delighted, to polite, and finally to sullen. I had struck out before the night had even begun. As we left to watch our movie, Muna made fun of me for trying the same lame joke twice. "Seriously dude, you are just not smooth. Better get on the aunty connection quick because you need help."

It was true. I needed divine intervention if I was going to be successful with the ladies. To AwkwardMan's delight, we ran into the same group of friends again after the movie. I wasn't stupid enough to try humor as an icebreaker again, so I kept it simple this time, using techniques I learned after Googling "How to talk like a normal person and not be weird."

I had noticed Zaiba right away. She was beautiful and had a good vibe: cool and down-to-earth. After the movie, as we all stood around talking, I happened to find myself next to her. Without overthinking it, I asked her and her friend if they were going to get dessert with the rest of the group. But, as the large group struggled to select a place, Muna and Zaiba's friends decided to go back to Muna's apartment.

"Want to tag along?" asked Muna.

"Yes. Yes I do," I said, in accordance with my recent resolution.

AwkardMan was kept rigorously in check that evening. Somehow, by the grace of the Big Man himself, I was able to start conversations with simple opening lines. And to my surprise, this continued successfully for the next couple of hours.

"You went to the same college as me? The same major? At the same time?" These were the highlights of my first conversation with Zaiba. AwkwardMan wanted to shout, "Where were you this whole time, you lovely person?!" Thankfully he mostly stood aside, only briefly making an appearance when, after talking for a while, I asked Zaiba how she spelled her name—my go-to question when I forget a person's name but am too embarrassed to admit it. I hadn't really been listening when we first chatted—she was distractingly good looking and I was busy thinking of the next half-interesting thing I could say to keep the conversation flowing.

"Z-a-i-b-a? That's so close to my name!" I said excitedly.

"Uh-huh, you mentioned that when we met earlier this evening," Zaiba replied.

Ah, AwkwardMan, you've had your bit of fun. Now please retire for the evening, I pleaded.

Zaiba seemed a little too good to be true. Beautiful, smart, funny, *and* willing to talk to me? This looks promising, I thought to myself. When this had happened in the past, my mind had quickly moved from "This girl is cool" to "I should definitely marry her, my whole life has been leading up to this point, don't screw it up!" That would generally be when AwkwardMan would appear and I would screw it up. But Zaiba was so easy to talk to that I just felt like myself. She made conversations easy and fun.

The next day, Muna asked me if I'd had a good time the previous night, with a raised eyebrow and wink. That's when I realized it was all part of a setup, casual but effective.

"Zaiba is really cool. We should hang out with her again," I replied.

"Oh, yeah?" she replied. "A few of us were having lunch next weekend if you want to join us."

Again, I said yes.

Saying yes was starting to become a habit in all areas of my life. Yes, I will go to lunch. Yes, I will take on that new project at work that I don't have any experience in. Yes, this girl is cool and interesting. And yes, I like her and want to get to know her better.

After lunch the next week we decided to walk around the mall. Muna and her friend walked a little bit ahead of us as Zaiba and I chatted. We were having a great conversation when out of nowhere we began talking about soccer and I insisted on showing her a cell phone picture of my new cleats.

"They're black on black!" I pointed out.

Zaiba politely agreed that they were indeed an excellent choice. A moment later, I realized what had just happened. AwkwardMan had made an appearance. No girl should be subjected to an extended conversation about the benefits of Adidas Predator soccer cleats, their history, and the list of famous players who wear them. But Zaiba hadn't reacted with a weird look or a shocked response. She accepted my awkwardness warmly, never made me feel stupid, and carried on as though things were normal.

I asked if she wanted to hang out together soon afterward. And, when that went well, we hung out again. Then, I randomly called her on the phone while she was out of town and soon we were hanging out often and talking every day. Each time we saw each other it felt a little better than the last. Within a few months, I realized I'd fallen completely in love with her. I loved her sense of calm, the way she treated her friends and family with such importance, and the care and effort she made in those relationships. I loved our conversations and the fact that AwkwardMan no longer had to be a secret identity. He was a part of me, and I finally accepted him as a personality quirk.

There were moments when we talked about my past, about how it had altered my outlook on life and how I was still in some ways rebuilding myself. But I was well on my way to a complete recovery, especially since Zaiba accepted me as I was, AwkwardMan and all. It was the most cared for I'd ever felt. For the first time in a long time, I allowed a good thing to happen to me.

Exactly a year after we first met, I took Zaiba to the place where we had had our first dinner. We ate our *shawarmas*, grabbed a selection of cupcakes, and headed over to Seal Beach. As we sat down, I took out something from the picnic basket I had brought with me. It was a jigsaw puzzle made up of photographs from our year together, including ones of an evening cruise around Newport Harbor, our fantastic time at Griffith Observatory, and the time I took her to see an LA Galaxy soccer game.

As Zaiba started piecing the puzzle together, I thought about how selecting the photos had given me a deep appreciation of our relationship. As she finished, I took out the last two pieces of the puzzle from my pocket. I said the words written on the pieces as I completed the puzzle: "Will you marry me?"

It was the moment my life had been building up to—as though the pain I had experienced was just one part of the Big Man's carefully designed plan. That pain made me grateful for the woman who accepted me as I was, and with whom I could share conversations, uncontrollable laughter, and even some lovely and awkward moments. Zaiba was the missing piece in the puzzle of my life, and I loved her dearly.

I waited, wanting to hear the same word that had changed my life and taken me from brokenhearted solitude to a happy life.

She said yes.

In the Unlikeliest of Places

By A. Khan

"Water, stories, the body,
All the things we do, are mediums
That hide and show what's hidden."

—Jalāl ad-Dīn Muhammad Rūmi

It was a sunny autumn day in New York. I was twenty-four years old. As my parents' marriage talk had heated up, I'd started feeling sickeningly guilty, knowing we were on different wavelengths.

I broke the news to my family on the phone, my hand held by a friend as we stood in a quiet Manhattan high-rise stairwell. I did want to marry—but it was probably going to be to a man, not a woman. This was my truth, and in sharing it, the anxiety that had ballooned inside me burst open. Even as my mother shouted that I would be ensured a spot in hell and then hung up, my body and my mind felt lighter and clearer.

Though shaded with a similar, palpable sense of loss, my father's response was different. Instead of quoting the Qur'an or threatening hellfire, he simply said, "Oh. Is marriage between men allowed in New York? Well, we will talk about it later. But I love you no matter what!"

Neither of my parents had been strictly observant for the majority of their lives. I was raised with a connection to my Islamic lineage, but never taught to root myself in an exclusivist or rigid interpretation of what being Muslim meant. While there were general guidelines, being "good" was implemented on a case-by-case, contextual basis.

I went through the prescribed ritual prayers mechanically as a child. They only started making sense as a spiritual practice of acceptance and gratitude during college. Even then, it seemed like it was a marker of identity as much as an act of devotion, and if I knew one thing, it was that my identity was not exclusively rooted in simple acts such as these.

For a couple of months after the phone call, I was strong. I was able to meet my parents' confusion and heaviness with love. *Would I tell anyone else in the family?* No one else needs to know for now, I suppose. *Had I become confused by hanging out with the wrong people?* Working overtime at a clinic where coworkers bonded during happy hour and commuting from the gentrifying neighborhood of Washington Heights, I was not part of a Muslim community—and after all, I *had* attended a liberal arts school. *And what of the girl I had been in a relationship with for over three years?* I had experienced the deepest love with my girlfriend. It was that love that had helped me become more myself, and helped me see my limitations, strengths, and desires more clearly.

I no longer fit the "good eldest son" role for my family. This turn of events I hadn't thought out. Inevitably, my heightened sense of clarity faded. I had thought that going through a "coming out"—like most good, queer American men of my generation—was enough. Courageous enough, illuminating enough, powerful enough. What I had invited my family into, I soon realized, was a tangled web of displacement. The unease I felt with myself did not go away, and doing the "right thing" by coming out started to feel hollow. It became harder day in and day out to walk a path of uncertainty, in the most fundamental of my relationships. My family, no matter what, was the beginning and the end of all the love in my life.

My mother cited God's words, but I did not feel any other participation of the divine in my life. I also couldn't be myself in my social landscape, whether of my extended family, the larger Muslim community, or my coworkers. Each of these groups understood some part of me, but no one got the whole picture.

When I still drank, I would visit bars and frequent websites that allowed me quick hookups with nearby men. Perhaps because of the seeming randomness to these interactions in a big city drunk on anonymity, and because of the cloud of silence generally associated with hookup culture, which privilege sexual fulfillment as the primary force in human relationships, there was little to guide me in unearthing and building human meanings from these experiences. I certainly did not think Allah had anything to say to someone who was looking for absolution without sacrificing the crutches of hooking up and drinking that kept me going in the loneliest of times. Life went on like this for a couple of years; I became immured in a false sense of perpetual crisis because of the very crutches that had initially helped me dull the pain of feeling fragmented in my identity, pulled apart by seemingly irreconcilable frameworks.

In the summer of 2010 I was at a point where loneliness, endorphin cravings, and a young man's testosterone overdrive collided and meshed together often—at least once a week, usually on the weekends. One rainy afternoon, I logged on to a dating/hookup site with a few movements of my fingers, wanting to be with someone.

I was in for a fun two hours: this was a particularly vibrant log-on session. I had multiple conversations going, and the temporary glow that came with feeling desired was in full flush as I flirted and calculated my way toward a "date." Eventually, I settled on an olive-skinned, silver-haired man whose ethnicity box was checked "Middle Eastern" and who lived on a fancy block a bit south of me. I did not make much of his Middle Eastern connection—he could have been Arab, Persian, Israeli, or lying—but he did have the right time line in mind: meeting as soon as possible.

I got myself ready and, excited by the unknown, got on and off the train in fifteen minutes. There was also a glow inside me from the awareness that *I did not have to wait.* How much your body feels it can fly in such moments, how much I would later wish I could freeze such moments in my life for future use. It was a nice walk to his building from the train stop. I previously had had little reason to visit this residential block of real houses and storied apartments in a city teeming with characterful patches. My senses tingling, I passed the doorman and realized that my date lived in the penthouse.

It turned out that he was a physician who worked downtown. He opened the door with a smile. The living room seemed like it was from the eighties, with its old TV, couches, and rugs like those my parents had at our home. The medium-size television was tuned to an Arabic-language station. What happened between my entering and the sex is absent from my memory now, but what we did in bed I can vividly recall. I remember being kissed on the couch, and that the kissing was smooth, and that it continued for a long time as we were lying down in bed. There were few words exchanged, as if our bodies might be enough for that afternoon.

A couple of hours later, I was silent and spent. He got up from the bed and put on some hot water for tea in his kitchenette. He then went to take a shower. I, for some reason, refused the offer to join him or take one separately, sitting back on the couch with my clothes on. When he came out fully dressed, he was smiling. It was time to water his plants, he said. But, after handing me a mug of steaming water along with some honey, he brought out a prayer rug from his bedroom, and started to perform *asr*.

I sat on the couch behind him, sipping my tea as he went through his prostrations. I started to become aware that I had been out of my body even when I thought I had been in it. I was observing myself even now, imagining how bizarre this scene might look to someone who *really* understood what it meant for me to not be praying. Even my nonobservant father had taught me that it was special to have the chance to pray in communion with others. I found myself wanting to join him by the end of his prayers. But I was still too stunned that this man was adding prayer to our "hookup" time together.

Afterward, I helped him water his plants—his wraparound balcony was covered and lined with them.

"I was raised Muslim. My mother was French, and I grew up in Brazil and some other places, as my father was a Lebanese diplomat," he said.

"Sounds like an interesting life."

"You have no idea. Are you hungry?"

I was.

"I'll make you a sandwich."

He toasted some bread on a pan and then spread butter and marmalade on it. He didn't have any himself. After putting on his glasses, he sat down with his own mug of tea and I returned to the couch to chew on the simple meal. I too had grown up across continents, but we were of different generations, and I wasn't sure what to make of this commonality. I did not feel, at the moment, very interesting, in contrast to the confidence of my older host.

Instead of opening up about my family, I talked about what was the bulk of my life and another point of intersection with his: my job. I worked as a patient liaison, and he was a doctor who had anatomy and physiology textbooks adorning his living room bookcases. He sounded like he had fun with his work; in any case, he worked only three days a week at his private practice. I was near the bottom of the pecking order at my office and perennially close to wanting to quit. My latest challenge was that Ramadan was now cycling into the summer months. While I had always had fun fasting, I worried that the demands of my workplace and the dehydration I already suffered from would be exacerbated by the ritual.

"Not at all! You will be all right," the man said. "Tell me about everything that worries you about it." He had answers to all my objections, and told me that despite the pressures of his life, he had fasted each year after his first time doing so in childhood. There was nothing, he exclaimed with a smile, that could get in the way of my being as good a Muslim as I wanted.

At some point soon after, it was clear we were no longer in the afternoon but in the shadow of dusk, and that "tea time" was over. I hadn't been magically transported into a *dars* or an imam's office; he had some work to do, he said, pointing to a stack of paper. He also "would be happy" to see me again, but there was only a week left until Ramadan, and he tended to not hook up during the month.

Perhaps we could meet again in what remained of the month of *Shaban*, or we could meet for *iftar* during Ramadan.

"Great meeting you!" he said with a parting kiss.

I headed back down the elevator and past the doorman for an early-evening "walk of shame."

After I left, I thought, *"What am I here for but for this?"* It was an oddly expansive sentiment to have for something that in the big picture was so complicated that I could not even relate the experience to another person in a straightforward way. Who does one even share something like this with?

I would not see him again in person, though I stayed on the dating site I had met him through and would see him pop up once in a while. He tried to get in touch once, but I did not know what to do with a man who was this much older than me; I did not want a "daddy" to take care of me. I needed to feel the comfort of my own father and mother. I could not even wrap my mind around the idea that I had begun some sort of relationship, when our meeting had been, for me, about seeking transcendence through escape, not connection.

Ultimately, our encounter was a lesson in the power of intention that I had failed to learn until then; while fortuitous incidents happen to us and around us all the time, and while we can always get fresh chances, the root intent of our actions matters. I had lost the ability to cultivate good intention for its own sake during the time that my relationship with my role models—my parents—had become one fraught with fear and guilt. I reawoke to this after that rainy summer afternoon, as I began to question my willingness thus far to accept myself as someone who was destined to lead a fragmented, compartmentalized life.

That said, I was also reminded of the love that was inside of my vivid desire for men, something that was easy to forget when it was an objectless and generalized desire, when it was seen as an aberration or something purely hormonal by so many. A common way to belittle same-sex models of love and marriage is to call them nonprocreative. This simplification fails to deal with all the little miracles this love can give birth to in the lives of people who have already been born.

Meeting the nameless man that day did that for me, and I only knew him for a blink of an eye. It takes repeated shocks to the system of those who are dependent on a drug—instead of being fully dependent on themselves—to remind themselves that they are alive and vulnerable and that this is not incidental to the playing out of something transcendent within the mundane. Never before meeting him had I met another Muslim who could pair his sexuality and piety in this way. It was the beginning of the end for me of the separation of the two. I had discovered that if these things could be reconciled, even in quiet ways hidden in the midst of giant metropolises, so too could I be reconciled to my parents.

He helped show me that the key to my salvation, so to speak, could be in building community with others in similar situations. A new wave of LGBTQ Muslim advocacy was cascading in the U.S. and across the world. In New York City, I eventually cofounded a meetup group for LGBTQ Muslims. When my new "family" began to expand with good souls I met through this work, I was able to start reforging my relationship with my birth family. In the slow grind toward full mutual acceptance, my parents and I are agreed that, at least, our communication had never been more honest.

The year 2010 also marked my first summertime Ramadan. While I had always fasted during Ramadan, I started to see prayer as an important, defining aspect of the month, and of daily life, after that encounter with the nameless man. The cliché that God works in mysterious ways becomes real only when you wake up to these mysterious ways in the small moments, in the unexpected and, yes, dark places. Love, and wholeness, emerge in and from places where society says they aren't supposed to.

Planet Zero

By John Austin

I was in Tokyo again after five years, sitting in a quaint café in the bustling district of Ikebukuro called "Planet Zero." I'd made a habit of frequenting this particular place on the weekends despite the long train ride from my neighborhood. I had come to Japan so I could be anonymous. My search for my own brand of Muslim-ness had derailed back in the States, and in the eight years since my conversion I'd found neither peace nor fellowship.

A close friend of mine from college had been running her own company, providing educational services to autistic children, and was in need of managerial experience. I'd been running my own design agency for some time, but decided to help make her company profitable. My business partner and I decided I should take a leave of absence in the hopes of eventually expanding our own business in Asia. I was in my early thirties and felt ready to take on an executive role. I also needed a change. Where else was an African American Japanese Muslim convert to find perspective?

Most weeks I left the house at 6 a.m. and didn't return until the last train, close to midnight—if I returned at all. The Planet Zero café, despite becoming part of a larger routine, broke up monotonous days and endless hours. There were no westerners there, which was my primary criterion for frequenting it. If there were no westerners, there would be no conversations in English. No conversations meant no exchanges of information, no e-mails, no end to my anonymity.

Planet Zero faced an alleyway. On the other side of the alley were old apartment buildings and various small shop fronts. The street side of the building appeared to be abandoned and I passed it several times before discovering, quite by accident, the alley that led to the coffee house. It was the difficulty in finding this place that provided me with the sense of comfort.

After I'd frequented the coffeehouse for nearly three months without incident, a woman walked in. She was dressed in business attire and wearing a pair of designer sunglasses. She was visibly startled by my presence. I couldn't see her eyes, but I knew she was looking at me. After a few seconds, her surprise at seeing a black man in an obscure coffeehouse faded, and she approached the counter.

She was carrying a large purse, from which she produced a wrinkled piece of torn legal paper. She began to speak unintelligibly to the barista, who obligingly nodded and smiled. I watched for several minutes, as she tried desperately to summon enough Japanese to make herself understood, before finally deciding to get involved.

"Miss? Maybe I can help you."

She turned to me, flustered, disheveled. A thin layer of sweat had formed on her forehead from the summer heat.

"Thank God. Someone who speaks English. Do you speak Japanese as well? I am trying to find this place." Her English was perfect but she spoke with an accent. She handed me a poorly drawn map and an address. I didn't know the area well since I typically came straight from the train station to the coffeehouse. I turned to the barista and asked him if he knew the address. Relieved, he began to tell me where the map had gone wrong.

"Once you are back on the main street, go left and walk for three blocks," I told her. She thanked me, took the paper from my hand, and left.

I didn't expect to see her again but hoped I would. Two weeks later I went back to the coffeehouse. She was there, hunched over her laptop, sipping a latte. I waited a few seconds for some sign of recognition before finding a place to sit. She was different that day, casual, relaxed. The only available seat was at a table right next to her. This was either going to be fortuitous or awkward. I found myself wanting to interact with her, though not for the obvious reasons. When I thought about it I felt a mixture of alarm and disappointment. The thing I tried to avoid by coming here was the thing that I most wanted at that moment: a conversation.

The barista brought me a latte. I was about to settle in for an afternoon of writing when I saw from my periphery that her head had turned in my direction. She cocked her head slightly and her mouth opened as if she was about to speak. I pretended not to see so that my own desperation would not become apparent. She began typing again, sipped her drink, and then stopped. Again she turned to face me and this time managed to speak.

"I thought I might run into you here."

I tried to hide my surprise at her candor. These days you can't say anything like that, man or woman, without appearing a bit *stalkery*. Of a dozen things I thought she might say, that wasn't close to any of them.

"Oh yeah?" I responded, which was followed by several seconds of us staring awkwardly at one another.

"Yes. I realized that I'd left without properly thanking you. It must have seemed quite curt and maybe a little rude."

"No worries. You seemed to be in a hurry. I didn't take it personally," I lied.

That conversation continued for several hours. Her name was Rana and she was a physician from Canada taking a course in world health at the University of Tokyo. As we closed out the coffeehouse she asked if I would help her with her Japanese because she was struggling in her class. My heart sank a little. I'm not sure what I was expecting, but our interaction had suddenly become less personal. I agreed to help her and we exchanged information.

Only a couple of days passed before she contacted me. I was leaving my office for a meeting, and it was turning out to be a particularly bad week at work. I wasn't in the mood to tutor her. She asked if I was free that evening and I let her know that my workday rarely ended before 10 p.m. Despite my persistent feelings of dejection about the turn our interaction had taken, I was determined to be an adult about it.

I asked myself: What are you expecting? In the U.S. it isn't often that you see an Arab woman and a black man together. Part of the reason for my flight from the U.S. was my disaffection over the state of my life as a Muslim. I had fallen off the "Muslim Wagon," and my spiritual and social pursuits had ground to a screeching halt. I found myself isolated, with only the judgments of my supposed peers to keep me company. I had interacted with many flavors of Muslims and most of those interactions were disappointing. To some I was not strict enough. With them I faced accusations that I craved secular life because I maintained my pre-Muslim friendships and I'd gone on dates with women. Certainly I wasn't holding out for a *rishta*. Why, then, invite more disappointment into my life?

"If you aren't too tired after you finish work, would you like to meet for coffee or a late meal?"

"I'm sorry, Rana, I don't think I can tutor you tonight. It's been a rough week and I don't have the energy."

"Oh no. I guess I wasn't clear," she interjected. "I assumed we would do that on the weekends. I just wanted to see if you wanted to meet up."

I took the phone away from my ear and eyed the handset with a puzzled look. I quietly pumped my fist and mouthed the word "yes!"

"Oh . . . of course," I replied.

I recommended a place we could go in Shibuya and asked her to meet me at the station's entrance. No sooner had I hung up the phone than my previous doubts crept into my head. I tried desperately to stave off any notions that this might be a date. After all, Japan could be a lonely place for anyone, let alone someone whose grasp of the language was, at best, remedial. But no matter how hard I tried I couldn't escape the anticipation or the giddiness. I was genuinely looking forward to seeing her.

We met that evening in Shibuya. And then three times a week over the next two weeks. I was reserved and stoic most of the time. There were times when I showed her a more personable side, but I often quickly restrained myself when the interaction became too familiar. We didn't meet once to study Japanese and yet I was steady in my belief that her interest was platonic. My status as a Muslim didn't play into my reservations. It was a fear that I had that perhaps I was completely misreading the situation. It was a fear of rejection.

The outings to Shibuya had become ritual. There was an area near the station that sat in the shadow of a bunch of "love hotels" that had the best food in the city. Every time we went out, we chose a different place and we would talk well into the night. On occasion the sun would be rising when we left. One particular night she seemed a little down. When I asked her if everything was okay, she said yes and we continued talking. I asked her a couple more times during the course of the evening, and the last time she became visibly frustrated.

"I wish you would stop asking me that. I'm fine."

There it was. The word. *Fine.* Internally I began kicking myself. We ate in silence for about half an hour, after which she said she wasn't feeling well and wanted to go. I'd been silently berating myself; now I began to panic.

I paid the tab and offered to walk her home. She said she would be fine; she would get a cab. My panic accelerated as she waved a taxi over. I knew if I let her get into that cab, I would never see her again. I didn't have time for self-flagellation, or doubt. It hadn't been my style, but if I let things go down this way I was going to have to wear it for a long time.

"Wait." I came up behind her as she was opening the door to the cab. I took her hand and turned her toward me. "What is going on with you?" I asked.

Without turning away she responded. "You."

I felt like a giant ass even before the word left her mouth. I made her say it, when I should have been the one. It should have been my neck hanging out there in the cool Tokyo air. But it wasn't. Even as I pulled her closer to me I was numb with disbelief. She put her arms around my neck and laid her head on my chest. We stood there in Dogenzaka Square, embracing in the shadow of love hotels. When I got up the nerve I pulled away just far enough to kiss her. I was breathing a sigh of relief into her.

Two weeks after that night in Shibuya, we were on the bullet train together rocketing toward Osaka at nearly three hundred miles per hour. Our relationship had progressed quickly, to the point where we were staying over at each other's apartments. I had my reservations about what was happening, but those reservations, again, had nothing to do with religion. They didn't have anything to do with being ambiguous about commitment either. I knew, as we relaxed into each other, that I wanted to be with her. But I didn't know if that was what she wanted. I couldn't broach the topic without either appearing overeager or demonstrating a fear of commitment.

I decided to let it play out. She was leaving in a few weeks and wanted to see more of the country. I took some time off from work so that we could hit Nagoya and Osaka together on a little getaway. We had a week together. The topic was bound to come up. I was simply reluctant to ruin the mood. Why shouldn't I be reluctant? I was happy. I wouldn't say that I loved her, but I certainly saw that potential. I cared enough for her to know that I wanted to follow this to the end. In my mind I even crafted ridiculous disqualifying criteria: *Wanted by Interpol*, or *trying to harvest my organs.* Those were the only two things I could think of that would make me not want to be with her.

At the last minute we decided to make a stop in Nara, the birthplace of my mother. I thought it would be a nice change from all the big-city stops we were making. We jumped off the bullet train and took a local line into Nara. It was already after noon when we arrived so I made arrangements for us to stay there that night. After a day of sightseeing and shopping we made our way to our accommodations, a tiny bungalow outside the city. It was almost rural.

Our lovemaking that night was particularly passionate. It was as if we both sensed the end of our time together in Japan and wanted as much of each other as we could have. We both drifted off to sleep. I awoke in the middle of the night because I was too hot. I got up, careful not to wake her, and stepped outside into the chilly summer air. The moon was full and I didn't need any other light. I sat on the porch of the bungalow, crossed my arms over my knees, and rested my head there. I knew where I wanted this path to go, but the way forward was obfuscated by unanswered questions. My heart had been beating so fast these last weeks, and yet it was heavy.

I heard her stir, followed by the sound of her feet padding across the wooden floor. The door creaked as she opened it. She immediately came behind me and knelt so she could lay her head on my shoulder. Her onyx hair spilled over my shoulder and I took in its scent.

"What are you doing out here?" she said softly and sleepily into my ear.

"Thinking."

"About what?"

"About us."

She came around and sat on the porch step next to me. "What about us?"

I remembered the night we first kissed. I wasn't going to let this conversation go down like that. There could be no stalling or rationalizing. I wanted her to know.

"I'm here. I'm not going anywhere." She looked at me quizzically. "I'm in this. All the way. For you." She stood up and held out her hand, which I took.

"Of course you are, silly. So am I. Now come back inside. I'm cold."

I was shocked. Was it possible I was overthinking it all this time? It appeared so. I followed her back to bed, where she curled up next to me. Her skin was still cold from the night air. I fell asleep and got some of the best rest I'd had in a while.

Everything became easy after that conversation, or rather more organic and natural. I felt free to really experience the happiness that had been bestowed upon us. We talked about life after Japan, and she was pleased that I was flexible. The details were never decided, but I was willing to muddle through a long-distance relationship until more-permanent arrangements could be made. In my mind "more-permanent" meant marriage. Quebec was only a few hours from DC by plane, and we decided on a tentative visitation schedule. We discussed how we would stay in touch, and how frequently we could realistically see each other. But there was one more hurdle to overcome.

On our way back to Tokyo she told me her parents were coming to visit her in her last week here. They had never been to Japan and wanted to see her and the city before she left. She asked if I would meet them. I could sense her reticence and nervousness when we discussed it. In her mind this was something that was unavoidable, and was best to get out of the way. I didn't have to be a genius to figure out what that meant. But I meant what I'd said to her in Nara.

Two weeks later I stood at the entrance to the suite on the fiftieth floor of the Park Hyatt Tokyo. From the other side of the door I could hear hushed yet emphatic words in Arabic, which only served to heighten my anxiety. I suddenly felt foolish holding a bouquet of flowers and other assorted gifts. Were it not for the air conditioning vent directly above me, I might have sweat through my shirt and jacket. After some shushing the door opened and an older woman, whom I guessed was Rana's mother, stood there with her best attempt at a smile, beckoning me in. I handed her the flowers.

"*Asalaamu alaykum,*" I managed to say while trying to swallow. Suddenly my throat was dry.

She struggled to maintain her smile and reciprocated the greeting halfheartedly, as if not expecting to have to say it. I followed her into the common area of the suite, where two men sat. The man I assumed was Rana's father sat scowling in an armchair in front of a floor-to-ceiling window. The other man, her brother, well groomed and in his twenties, sat on an adjacent love seat trying his best not to meet my gaze. In the distance behind them I could see the treetops of Shinjuku Central Park. Suddenly I wanted to be anywhere but here. There was some commotion to my right, down the hallway to the living area, but I did my best to ignore it.

I steeled myself and entered the common area, ushered in by Rana's mother. She offered me a seat opposite the men. I paused and extended my hand to Rana's father, which he took. I removed the gift I had brought for him and offered the obligatory greeting again: "*Asalaamu alaykum.*" Like the mother he reciprocated, but it was much more practiced. He took the gift in his hand and eyed it with what seemed like suspicion before unceremoniously tossing it onto an end table next to what appeared to be a glass of scotch. I turned to the younger man and offered my salutations for a third time before taking the seat I'd been offered.

"This thing with you and my daughter must end." My butt had barely hit the seat when her father started. This *thing?* I maintained my composure but remained silent for some time, considering how to respond. Meanwhile, Rana had appeared from the living area, her eyes swollen and red. She walked awkwardly past me and sat next to her brother and mother on the loveseat.

"I did not come here to be dictated to," I said. "And certainly not to be insulted."

"I don't care why you came here!" he shouted. "I know you will not leave with what you came for!"

"Baba—" Rana began, but she was stopped by her father's icy stare.

"I've come here out of respect," I said. "But the decision I will abide by is Rana's. If she tells me it is not possible for us to be together, then I will respect her wishes." I turned to look at her. Her head hung, and I saw tears running from her cheeks to her hands, which she was wringing in her lap.

"Rana, who is this man?" her father said. "What do you know about him? Where is his family from? I doubt if he even knows!" The implication could not have been any more clear, and though I was insulted, I held my tongue. I wanted to tell him that he was wrong, that I did know the origins of my family, that I came from generations of educated and successful people. But I didn't. My anger wouldn't allow it. I was a black man being judged for being black, or, at the very least, for not being Arab. All of those things I wanted him to know, I suddenly didn't want to say. I cared for Rana. I loved her. But what kind of man would she be getting if I bowed to this kind of behavior?

"Is he even a good Muslim?" he asked. I eyed the glass of scotch next to my discarded gift.

After a long and anxious silence fell over the room, Rana spoke. "I think you should go, John."

I felt the blood drain from my face. The father's countenance remained impassive. I didn't say anything. I couldn't. I had only enough life and will in me to stand, button my jacket, and walk toward the door.

"Have a good evening." I walked from the common area and to the door. There was complete silence even as the door closed behind me. I continued slowly toward the elevator, trying to comprehend what had happened. Part of me wanted to give Rana a chance to come sprinting down the hallway after me. She didn't.

I called and e-mailed her a couple of times after that. I was hoping to catch her at a time when she was clear of the influence of her father. I guess such a time never came. We never spoke to or saw each other again.

How Did I End Up Here?

By Arif Choudhury

"Any dates lined up, Ma?"

"No."

I was exhausted. After almost thirty hours of travel I finally arrived in Dhaka, the capital of Bangladesh. I took a nap, woke up, and was now talking to my mother, who had arrived two weeks earlier to visit relatives.

"Am I meeting any girls?"

"No."

"What? None?"

"There are no dates."

I was disappointed. I had come to Bangladesh to take care of family business, visit relatives, and reconnect with a country that I loved to visit as a child. While I was here I had also hoped *to meet my future bride.* That last part sounded odd when I thought it. How did I end up here?

Before I was born, my parents immigrated to the U.S. from what is now Bangladesh. I grew up in the northern, majority-white suburbs of Chicago. As the eldest child in an immigrant family I realized that my parents couldn't teach me everything about America so I turned to television. It seemed like the most dependable source of information and I watched countless hours. Like the other boys in the neighborhood, my favorite shows were *Knight Rider* and *The A-Team.* I developed crushes on the women I saw, including Wonder Woman and Jeannie—one had an invisible jet and a golden lasso while the other one could grant wishes! My more age-appropriate affections were focused on Punky Brewster.

When I wasn't watching TV, I daydreamed. Often, I'd wonder what it would be like to be a grown-up like my father. Being a grown man meant having a job, being married, and raising a family. Sometimes, I imagined being married to Wonder Woman. I later learned that Wonder Woman was really an actress named Lynda Carter. So, I then imagined I'd marry Lynda Carter. But she was over twenty years older than me. If I couldn't marry Lynda Carter, I imagined the next best thing: I'd marry a woman like her. I'd marry a white woman.

This was easier said than done. In Islamic Sunday school, the uncles and aunties were teaching me to be a good, practicing Muslim. I learned about the life of the Prophet and the lives of the *Sahabah*, about *fiqh* and shariah. They told me that Muslims weren't supposed to date as they do in the West, that sex was for after marriage and so were other forms of physical affection. I wanted to be a good Muslim, so I avoided dating in high school. Even while I was being bombarded with images of love, romance, and sex in TV, movies, music, and literature, I knew that to be a good Muslim boy I must avoid romantic, physical relations with girls.

During senior year in high school, I was walking through the hallway between classes when Mary stopped me to ask, "How's Beth doing?"

"I don't know. Fine, I guess. How should I know?"

"She told me that you two were going out."

"Wait, what? We're going out?"

I thought about it. A bunch of us would all go to the movies in a group, but the last few times I went to the movies it was only Beth and me. When she said, "Want to go to the movies?" I guess she had asked me out. I didn't know girls could do that. In the movies it seemed the guy always pursued the girl. Furthermore, I didn't know that girls might be attracted to me. Beth and I went out a few more times and I wasn't sure what to do now that we were *a couple*. Dating, like everything else, is a learned behavior and I didn't have any role models to teach me what to do. I was trying to be a practicing Muslim and I didn't want to sin.

Even though I liked it when Beth was physically affectionate toward me—holding my hand, hugging me, kissing me—I felt it was wrong. I didn't know how to act or what to say. I was awkward. So when Beth called me one night to ask, "What are we?" I replied using humor as a defense mechanism. "Umm . . . *Homo sapiens*?" Needless to say, she moved on. I was relieved.

When I got to college, I studied the mating rituals of the indigenous population—my college classmates—like a cultural anthropologist. I eventually figured it all out—how to tell if a girl likes me, how to ask her out, all of that. And when I did, I started looking for pretty girls—white girls—who liked the "right" books, movies, and music. It seems that I was searching for the female version of me. Trying to find "the one" while also trying to maintain my religious beliefs was a struggle.

If I was looking for the female version of me, why didn't I date an American-born Bangladeshi Muslim girl? Because they were inaccessible. Growing up in the Bangladeshi community in Chicago, all of us boys and girls were raised as though we were siblings or cousins. One of the uncles in the community once asked me, "Do you feel as though you can't marry the Bangladeshi girls you grew up with because you think of them as sisters?" "Exactly," I replied. "It feels incestuous. They aren't romantic possibilities. It's too weird. I've been calling all of you uncle and auntie. If I marry your daughter I'd be calling you Abba and Amma—it would be strange to have you as in-laws." *Besides, I thought, you are all so freaked out about dating, how are we supposed to couple up? You would all know if we were going out to the movies or for coffee . . . or who knows what else.*

Since our Bangladeshi Muslim parents wouldn't let us date, we all dated secretly—some sooner than others. We found boyfriends and girlfriends from outside the Bangladeshi Muslim community who *were* allowed to date. Because of this, a lot of the American-born Bangladeshis—both men and women—in my community began marrying outside our ethnic group and sometimes outside our faith.

By my early thirties, I realized that the aunties and uncles in my community wanted me to settle down. They feared that I might marry a non-Bangladeshi or worse—a non-Muslim. If I did, I'd be a bad role model for their children, who were younger than me.

The elders—including my mother, of course—began to be more proactive, asking, "When are you going to get married? I know a nice girl for you." At one Bangladeshi wedding I attended, an uncle sitting at the table with my parents suggested that I walk across the banquet hall and talk to a few unmarried girls. Wow! This was a drastic turnaround. When we were adolescents, there would be gossip about "dating" and how it could lead to "sin." Now, this uncle wanted me to actually pick up girls at a Muslim wedding?!

That wedding was a turning point. I was becoming disillusioned with dating white girls because issues of religion and culture would get in the way. The girls were great and open-minded, but often their family members weren't as enlightened. It got to be a drag when I had to explain multiple times to the father of one girlfriend that it was the holy month of Ramadan and I was fasting. "Are you still not eating?" he'd ask. "How long are you going to do this? It's ridiculous!"

I decided I wanted to find a girl who had similar religious and cultural values—a Muslim woman who was born and raised in the U.S. A woman of Bangladeshi descent would be all the better. But where was I going to find this woman? I didn't meet Bangladeshi Muslim women randomly. I had to be set up through aunties or through the *rishta* process, which I was wary of. Would I get to know the woman properly?

Despite the mechanical nature of the *rishta* process, I still hoped to fall in love with one of the girls that I talked to. This was the American part of me, the part that believed in romantic love—the part that grew up on *Romeo and Juliet*, *West Side Story*, *Fiddler on the Roof, When Harry Met Sally,* and dozens of pop songs about love and romance, from Elvis Presley to Michael Jackson.

At the same time, I believed in the love story that was my parents' marriage. My parents didn't have the standard Western romance—they didn't date before marriage, hold hands, and make goo-goo eyes at each other. After my father established himself as a physician in the United States, he returned to Bangladesh to marry. His aunts sent word to my mother's family that a Bangladeshi doctor from America had come back home to marry. My maternal grandfather thought my father seemed calm, polite, educated, and soft-spoken—the kind of man who would make a kind and gentle husband. My mother decided to let her parents choose for her—she figured that they knew better, and she also had faith that Allah would surely bring her a good husband. In our faith, marriage is not just about the love, infatuation, or attraction that the couple feels, but also a blending of tribes/families. It was decided that the two families were compatible. One week later my parents were married.

In marriage, they came to deeply love each other. I once heard a Muslim woman describe the difference in marriage customs between the East and the West: in the West, couples start off hot and then cool off, but in the East couples start off cool and then warm up. This is what happened for my parents, so I believed that it might be possible for me too. I prayed to Allah to find me a compatible wife/soul mate/life partner/best friend who was good for me. This prayer gave me the energy and the emotional strength to endure the challenging process of finding "the one."

Still, the *rishta* process wasn't easy. I was quickly rejected by many *ghotoks*, bachelorettes, and their parents because I was: short, over-weight, old (I was thirty-four when I started to take the process seriously), modest or frugal with respect to wardrobe, too Muslim, not Muslim enough, had artistic aspirations, was not an MD, MBA, or PhD, and was living at home with my parents (I stuck around to help my mother take care of my father while he was ill).

I was mostly talking to American-born Bangladeshi Muslim girls outside of Chicago because there were only three American-born Bangladesh girls in Chicago who were of an appropriate age for me. I wasn't interested in two of them and the third wasn't interested in me—because I was an artist, she was afraid we'd live a life of poverty.

The *rishta* process began to take a toll, with one rejection after another.

"Why don't you go back home and find a nice girl to marry?" my friend Farooq suggested. "When I was finally ready to marry, I went back home and found a nice, simple, religious girl—a good Muslim girl. I married her and brought her here to America."

That was easy for Farooq to say because he was born in Bangladesh. For me to marry a girl from Bangladesh would be more challenging. Would our different upbringings and life experiences lead us to want different things? Maybe she wouldn't want a career and would think life was all saris and gold bangles, dinner parties and shopping sprees, summers in Bangladesh visiting her parents instead of accompanying me on more culturally eye-opening trips to Johannesburg or Shanghai. Maybe she'd be shocked or annoyed if during a business dinner one of my clients ordered wine. Or, would she overcompensate like the girls from Bangladesh who learned to party hard, drink, and wear skimpy clothes?

How would I even get to know a girl from Bangladesh? I had spent the previous four years talking to Bangladeshi girls all over North America. It was hard enough to get to know them while juggling work, activities, and different time zones. How would I get to know a girl on the other side of the globe? And I definitely didn't want to be someone's only path to a green card!

"Would you marry a French girl?" a Bangladeshi friend asked.

"Well, yes, if she was hot! Joking aside, yes, I'd consider marrying a French girl if we shared the same values and passions in life."

"So, why not a girl from Bangladesh? All of your hesitations about a Bangladeshi girl would apply to a French woman too, no?" My friend had a point. When my mother and I found out we had to go to Bangladesh to take care of some property that I'd inherited, I told my mother to contact my cousin Shaju to set up some dates with eligible girls.

Shaju had assured me that, through her network of friends and *ghotoks*, she'd be able to introduce me to dozens of girls and that all I had to do was just say the word. But, Shaju helped me meet just one girl on that trip. As I was preparing for the end of my visit, Shaju told me that through one of her *ghotoks* she learned of a girl who was pursuing her MBA in Canada who happened to be visiting Bangladesh too; she was from a good family and was a good prospect. She also told me that the girl's family had inquired about me.

"Are you interested in meeting her?" Shaju asked.

"Sure."

Two days before returning to Chicago, Shaju, her older brother, Musa, his daughter Noor Jahan, and I drove to an upscale mall to meet The Girl and her mother. I wasn't even told The Girl's name. Noor Jahan was giddy. She was nine years old and felt very grown up for being invited. I love Noor Jahan, but she made me nervous. During my entire visit in Dhaka, she'd been poking my belly—I had a potbelly—and calling me "fatso." I had hoped to hide how heavy I was with my outfit, but wouldn't be able to hide it if during a conversation with The Girl, Noor Jahan poked me in the belly and I giggled like the Pillsbury Doughboy.

It was Ramadan, so none of us was eating or drinking, but the *ghotok* decided that we should all meet at a snack shop on the second floor of the mall. We arrived to find the *ghotok*—chubby, in her fifties, wearing glasses and a white *hijab*—sitting alone at one of the snack shop's dozen or so Formica tables. Shaju walked up to her first and gave her salaam. When I gave her my salaam, she looked me up and down and said, "You're not very tall." Ouch. I was in trouble. The *ghotok* hadn't known what I looked like—my heart sank.

I too had come to the date blind. I had no idea what The Girl looked like. But that was okay as I was desperate to meet someone

. . . anyone. But, if the *ghotok* didn't know what I looked like, that meant The Girl and her family didn't either. No matter how smart, witty, charming, or accomplished I was, she could reject me if she did not find me attractive. She might think that I'm fat. I am fat. Not horribly fat, but I could stand to lose twenty pounds or so. And, like the *ghotok* said, at five feet six inches I'm not very tall. Bangladeshis are not tall people, but everybody seems to want a tall groom for their daughter (maybe they're planning to breed the short gene out). Thank Allah that I wasn't bald!

We all stood up as they entered the snack shop. First, the brother of The Girl walked in and introduced himself. Then The Girl, her mother, and aunt walked in and sat down next to Shaju and the *ghotok*. The Girl was taller than me—at least five feet eight inches. She was wearing flip-flops to decrease her perceived height. Her mother stood for a while and stared at me, examining me as if I were a prize bull for sale. Her face crinkled up as though she smelled a bucket of rotten eggs. She gave me another glance and then sat down and whispered to the aunt. The men chatted among the men. The ladies chatted among the ladies. I noticed that The Girl giggled whenever I spoke in my American-accented Bengali. Soon it was all over. I didn't even get a chance to talk to The Girl! Neither the mother nor The Girl asked me any questions, which I took as an indication of uninterest. After the meeting, I told Shaju to call them and let them know that I was still interested. I wasn't, but she was still a prospect. Who knows, I thought, it might lead to something. It didn't.

After my trip to Bangladesh, I decided to try every method of dating possible—this was now a full-time job. I would use the *rishta* process, online dating, Muslim speed-dating, setups by friends and family, and attend events where young Muslim professionals congregate. The only way I was able to get through was by being hopeful that I might actually find "the one."

I am thirty-seven and single. And I'm trying to be okay with that. There is an advantage to being a single guy—I lead a pretty full life. I've shot documentary films in China and India, taught improv comedy in Beijing and Singapore, written short stories, films, plays, songs, and a children's book. I perform as a storyteller and stand-up comic all around the U.S. and also overseas. I work on social justice causes and build bridges between people of different faith traditions and cultural backgrounds. All of this is fun and exciting . . . but sometimes it feels less meaningful without someone with whom I can share these experiences.

There are constant reminders that everyone else is coupled up except me. I attended a Bangladeshi Muslim wedding in which the bride and the groom were both divorcees. Somehow they found each other. They were each on their second marriage, while I wasn't even on my first!

At times, I feel lonely and demoralized, worthless and as unappreciated as the last piece of chocolate in a Whitman Sampler. The appealing chocolates have been eaten. Most people have read my description and taken a pass. Or they took a bite out of me, didn't like my unfamiliar taste, and put me back in the box—half-eaten, alone, waiting to be thrown out.

My sister says I'm a catch. I know what she's trying to say—that I'm reasonably handsome, educated, well-spoken, funny, and fun to be with. I have a passion for life and I want to help people—I want to leave the world a better place than I found it. I have a keen knowledge of culture both high and low. I can quote Shakespeare and *The Simpsons*. I like Ravel and the Rolling Stones. I can wax intelligent on the West Coast offense and West Coast jazz. However, it's hard to think of myself as a catch when I've been single this long—when I just can't find "the one."

Still, I've got a full schedule this week. I've got a date with a girl I met online and a few more bio-datas have been e-mailed to me. I'm trying to be optimistic, but who knows what the future will bring?

Springtime Love

By Mohamed Djellouli

On my first date with Rabia, we met at a café in the early afternoon on a cold February day. We are graduate students in different programs at the same university in San Francisco. We had met only briefly once before, but our conversation was immediately engaging, flowing naturally from faith to family to politics. I couldn't help staring at her hands—half the time punctuating her sentences with Arab flourish, half the time wending through her long, curly hair. I found myself wishing I could be one of her fingers.

Our date went on for four hours without either of us noticing. This was a woman I could fall in love with, and since she was a Muslim woman, maybe I wouldn't have to feel guilty about it. My mind started to jump to all sorts of far-off questions: Where would we be married? What would our kids look like? What does she look like without—

Her phone buzzed loudly.

"Hi, Baba. . . . I'm in the library. . . . No, I don't need a ride. I'm going to take the train later. . . . Yeah, I just have an Arabic assignment I have to finish. . . . Don't worry, I'll be fine. . . . I'm almost done. . . . Okay. . . . Okay. . . . Okay. . . ."

I wasn't the only person on this date. Rabia had been glancing at her phone constantly as it buzzed with phone calls and text messages.

"Is everything okay?" I finally asked.

"Yeah, that was just my . . . father, mother, sister, and brother calling to check in on me."

The phone buzzed again. "I'm sorry, I have to take this."

I knew that dating a Muslim woman would not be without complications. I grew up Muslim, but not typically so. I'm mixed-race; my white mother is agnostic, while my North African father is more of a secular Muslim. I grew up in San Francisco, the only Muslim among my circle of friends, not really understanding what that meant beyond having a funny name. As a young person, my only dating concern was that I wasn't having more success picking up women.

Rabia, on the other hand, was a Lebanese American who grew up in the Gulf. And while her father and mother were relatively liberal for their family and social milieu, her baseline was far more religiously conservative than mine, especially when it came to dating. Her parents forbade her from ever spending time alone with men.

Despite our different backgrounds, religion was a subject over which we connected deeply.

As I grew older, I became more religious. I began spending more time visiting my very religious family in the homeland and found that faith gave purpose and direction to my life, illuminating the values and beliefs that I'd always held: in the purpose and value of every experience, in higher accountability for my actions, and in the necessity of serving others. But because my parents raised me without a rigidly traditional foundation, I was left with the freedom to build the principles of my religious practice on my own. I doubted that the typical Muslim woman would share my worldview.

Amazingly, Rabia met me from the other side of the forest. Raised in a traditional family and a conservative community, her personal exploration and questioning of her faith had brought her to similar views as mine, rooted in a deep love of God. But whereas I was free to start from scratch, she had to contend with a heavy set of assumptions and norms. Reconciling distinct moral landscapes and conducting oneself as a Muslim woman in a non-Muslim society was especially challenging when there were also family expectations. Our paths diverged upon the question of dating.

Rabia had dated before—short relationships with Muslim men spent tiptoeing around the community's scrutiny. I had much more dating experience. My first serious relationship, with a non-Muslim early in college, was a challenging experience, but I learned a lot from it. I fell in love with another non-Muslim as soon as I graduated from college. Our relationship was passionate, intense, and ill fated. We broke each other's hearts like colliding trains. By the end, I realized that I wanted to be with a Muslim. The way in which I viewed the world and wished to conduct my life, while reflective of my pluralist upbringing, was still decidedly Muslim. I wanted to be with someone who understood and inspired this side of me.

I was twenty-five the summer before I met Rabia. My second serious relationship had just ended, and I was returning home to attend graduate school—this was the perfect time to begin implementing the changes I wanted to see in myself. Beyond searching for a Muslim partner, I was eager to make the Muslim community the central part of my life while shedding the more complicated and isolating aspects of the constant in-betweenness of my identity and social circle.

I saw my first chance that summer when I had to find a new doctor. There were only two doctors taking new patients in my HMO, a Jewish woman and an Arab man. I signed up for an appointment with the Arab wanting to support a Muslim/Arab professional and to begin deepening my relationship with the community, even in this small way.

He was a Lebanese man with kind eyes and an open demeanor. Having seen my name, he immediately asked me where my family was from and what I did. And though he was proud to see an Arab boy getting a good education, he was a little disappointed that I didn't speak better Arabic. He spoke a little about his children and his hopes for them. Then he started asking me the routine medical questions.

"Do you smoke?"

"No." A subtle hint of approval.

"Do you drink?"

"No, sir." Again, approving.

"Have you been sexually active in the past six months?"

Shit. I paused. How do I answer? Maybe this whole mission of endearing myself to the community was going to be a lot harder than I thought. My past would not be easily shrugged off.

I had lost my virginity at eighteen. Sex had been a healthy and fun part of all of my relationships. Even as I became more disciplined in my practice of Islam, I had trouble throwing sex out. Instead, I ignored this inconsistency, passing my actions off in my mind as at worst a minor sin that, hopefully, would be forgiven. But I still avoided discussing it with any of my Muslim friends.

Should I lie? Was I even allowed to lie to a doctor? Why is he asking me these questions? Is this relevant? Should I tell him I used protection?

"Yes," I answered sheepishly.

His hesitation seemed laden with visible discomfort and disappointment as he looked down and silently scratched my answer onto his clipboard. He quickly moved on and checked my blood pressure, but my guilt lingered.

As I left his office I regretted not seeing the Jewish doctor. Had I really done something so wrong that this doctor should be ashamed of me? Growing up outside of the rigid confines and gossip networks of a Muslim community, and always keeping my private life close to my chest, I had been able to escape the shame and reprobation felt by many other Muslims who dated and had sex. If this was the reaction of a random doctor, how would the Muslim queen I was looking for react?

But when I tried to make myself regret my past actions, I couldn't. When I thought about my life and how much I had learned from my relationships, how beautiful a positive, healthy sexual connection could be, how frustrated and lonely so many of my Muslim friends were, it was hard to vilify the act. I was not going to argue that my sexual past was righteous, but I also wasn't going to beat myself up about it.

I met Rabia soon after at an event of the Justice for Palestine group at the university. Though I am all about the cause, that night I had just wanted to grab some falafel and return to studying. I soon forgot my plans when I laid eyes on this beautiful woman. She was graceful and radiant, with dark eyes that sparkled even from afar and long, curly hair that fell softly across her shoulders. I spent the next hour chatting with people as I worked my way across the room to her. We connected immediately and I secured a date for coffee right as the event was ending and she had to run home. Time pressure was part of our relationship right from the beginning.

We continued to see each other after our first date. She was sharp, political, and radiated a warmth and kindness that I found intoxicating. I was soon smitten. We moved slowly but inexorably toward each other. Our second date ended with a hug. Our fourth, with the slightest touch of our hands (my hand burned with her touch for hours afterward). We kissed on our fifth date. I spent those first weeks in a daze: laughing at seemingly random moments, smiling excessively, writing poetry, eagerly anticipating each meeting.

But the feeling that my past had left me tainted continued to plague me. One way I thought I could minimize the fallout over this truth with Rabia was to be sure that I carried no baggage from my past. It had been a year since I last got tested for STDs. I would have to return to my Arab doctor. Steeling myself, I defiantly made an appointment.

When I got to his office, there was no doubt that his discomfort outweighed mine. He quickly asked me background questions and sent me off to the lab. He called me a week later and tersely reported that my results were negative.

Rabia and I continued to get closer. By this time, we were having trouble keeping our hands off each other. She had been coming over to my house, and things were starting to feel noticeably sexual, though our clothes always stayed on and our hands remained above sea level. I was careful not to push the envelope.

Rabia lived at home, in the suburbs, and would be picked up by a family member early every evening to return home. She was never in the city on weekends. After our first date, her mother sensed that something was up, and accused her of having a secret boyfriend. I was used to relationships that were open and involved sleepovers and unbounded time. So I couldn't help but be frustrated at how much we had to tiptoe already. Yet it clearly wasn't enough. Every time we were together, she would receive calls and text messages from everyone in her family and would have to tell ever-more-elaborate lies. Compounding her guilt about deceiving her family was the feeling that during our make-out sessions we were doing something wrong, and it was all becoming too hard a load for her to carry.

And she still didn't know the extent of my history. I was putting off the inevitable conversation, not wanting to face up to the idea that I was somehow not worthy of this lovely angel.

One afternoon we were out at a café when, as usual, Rabia started looking at her phone, heralding yet another premature close to our time together.

"Can I walk you to the train?" I asked, slightly annoyed, but resigned to these inevitable abrupt departures. "I want to get in as much time as I can with you."

"No, my father is going to drive me home today. His clinic is right around the corner."

Fuck.

It dawned on me.

Rabia's father was my doctor.

I had known that her father was a doctor, but my stupid ass didn't know, didn't think, didn't realize . . .

They had the same last name, and how many Arab doctors could there be in this city?

Fuck.

After my date with Rabia, I went to meet my friend Farah. When I told her what I had figured out, she shouted, "No!!!!" and fell over laughing.

"At least you didn't get deep into this relationship."

"Wait, you don't think it's going to work out?" I asked.

More laughter.

"This is a good Muslim girl, who lives at home with her conservative parents, and her father is your STD doctor?"

"Yeah, so?"

"No, it's not going to work out, but don't worry, there are plenty of other Muslim women out there. If you are serious about this one, I wouldn't tell her. Just hope her father forgets you before she wants to get married."

I started to despair.

The next time Rabia and I hung out, we met at a café to do work.

"What are you reading?" I asked.

"A book on Sufism. I'm reading the chapter on sexuality. On how some classic scholars thought that sex was the most powerful means for connecting to God."

"Huh. Interesting . . ." I started sweating.

"The author is basically arguing that we too often vilify sex and label it as dirty without appreciating how it can be a powerful bond of love between people. Isn't that interesting?"

I had stopped paying attention. Why is she talking about sex? Does she know something? Is she testing me? I changed the subject.

"So, I was praying at *Jumma* yesterday, and this dude next to me fell asleep during the *khutbah*. Started snoring. Can you believe that? Ha-ha."

I needed advice, so I turned to my father. I hoped that his wisdom would prove more heartening than Farah's.

"Why should he care what you do?"

"He's her father."

"What a Muslim asshole. Let me tell you, everyone has sex. I left the village so I could do what I wanted. And when I was in Paris in the sixties, I was free, before I met your mother. Now you want to grow a beard and go back and marry some cousin? Let me tell you, all those assholes were having sex whenever they could. Now they all think they are too good for everyone and don't even know how to treat a woman with respect."

Damn. If my father didn't think my situation was a problem, then it was definitely a problem.

As I continued to see Rabia, her guilt and stress over dating and lying was building. And here I was, knowing full well that her father had seen my little Habib before she had. That he knew more about my sexual past than she did. That I knew her family better than she thought. I had to tell her.

We had been sitting at a little Indian restaurant for an hour, my attention distracted by thoughts of how to broach the fateful topic, when I finally worked up the nerve to plunge right in.

"So, I wanted to talk about our past," I paused. "I think it's important that we know where each of us has . . ."

She cut me off.

"Let me guess, you want to tell me that you've had sex."

"Wait, what?"

Did her father tell her? That Muslim asshole. Is this how we are going to end? Am I going to have to go back to dating non-Muslims?

"I assumed as much," she replied. "Everyone has sex, and you don't strike me as the 'virgin type.'"

Damn. I had been spending all of this time making assumptions about her, lumping her into my preconceived archetype of a typical Muslim woman. She clearly had spent that time actually listening to me.

"So . . . ?"

"Me? I've never had sex. My parents would kill me, and I want to wait until I am married anyway. But I would think it'd be kinda strange if you hadn't."

Well, okay then. But I couldn't help thinking what her parents, what her father would do if she ever brought me home. I hesitated before continuing.

"I have something else to tell you. I know your father." I told her, my legs shaking slightly underneath the table.

"Really? How?"

"He is my doctor."

"Really?" Her brow knitted in confusion.

"He's my . . . primary care doctor. . . . Really nice guy."

"Small world, but why didn't you tell me earlier?" she asked. At this point there was no reason for me to hide the ball.

"He knows I've had sex! He tested me for STDs!"

She started laughing.

"I sure hope it was negative," she said between laughs.

I paused, dumbfounded. I had spent all of this time building this up in my head as if it were an epic tragedy. Her patience and understanding made me ashamed of the lonely dialogue I had been having in my head without her. I should have brought this up weeks ago.

"It was," I finally fumbled out.

"Well, he isn't going to meet you anytime soon, so don't worry. He probably forgot you anyway."

I was still speechless. That went better than I thought. But, wait, how did he forget me? And why isn't he going to meet me anytime soon? I thought this was going somewhere . . .

Now it's May and the air is warmer. Rabia and I are still together and I have yet to run into her family. After our conversation, I committed myself to being more open and communicative. Finding time to be together continues to be a struggle, but now it's our shared struggle. I am slowly relinquishing my hang-ups and fear over what my past might mean in this relationship, and every day Rabia challenges my poorly conceived notions of how Muslim women think. She has made it clear that what matters most to her is who I am, not what I have done. We're dealing with the normal challenges of learning about each other and building love in complicated and busy lives.

I did, however, get a new doctor. The Jewish woman.

Finding Mercy

By Anthony Springer Jr.

I was born and raised Christian in Las Vegas—a modern-day Sodom and Gomorrah in the eyes of most religious people. Church never appealed to me. Sleeping in beat waking up for Sunday sermons, and Saturday-morning cartoons were infinitely better than the Song of Solomon. All I needed to know was that treating people as I wanted to be treated was the way to go, and that I'd get into heaven because Jesus died for my sins.

As an adventurous college kid, I racked up quite a few transgressions. Shortly after graduation, I took a hard look at my faith. That's when everything fell apart. I realized I didn't believe God had a son and that the Trinity made no sense to me. Christianity was like the dusty family photo album you never look at but immediately notice once it goes missing. I mourned my loss of faith, even though I hadn't cared much for the religion in the first place.

I knew I believed in one god—but that's all I knew. I believed in *tawhid* before I knew what the word meant. After a little research, I stumbled on Islam and felt like I had arrived at an oasis: No trinity. No savior. No original sin. Just me and Allah. Sign me up!

I didn't know anything else about Islam. I didn't need to. I drove down to a nearby *masjid* on a Wednesday. The imam's wife answered the door after three nervous knocks. In my haste to be cordial I extended my hand, which she reluctantly shook. She may have been as shocked at my gesture as I was to find out later that handshaking was considered improper between unrelated Muslim men and women. I told her I wanted to be Muslim, was introduced to some brothers at the *masjid*, and took my *shahada* after *Jumma*.

At the time of my conversion, in the fall of 2006, I was fresh out of college with my first job as a college recruiter at my alma mater, the University of Nevada, Las Vegas. I suppose a steady job and a degree made me a suitable candidate for marriage in the eyes of older brothers in the community, as it didn't take long for the "M" word to come up. I sheepishly brushed off most of the marriage conversations, opting for a smile and an *"inshAllah"* when asked when I was taking a step, which felt more like walking the plank than fulfilling half my *deen*.

After all, I was an eligible bachelor who still occasionally partook in the vices of life. And as a twenty-two-year-old, very Western convert, the idea that I was supposed to find the love of my life without "dating" was more foreign than the Arabic that penetrated my ears the first time I heard the Qur'an recited at the *masjid*. Then there was the pressure—the pressure on brothers to get married is as strong as the pressure put on sisters. Or so it was in my case. Equality and resistance made for strange bedfellows.

One day after *Jumma* I was caught staring aimlessly off into space, my peaceful state of bliss shattered by a gentle hand on the shoulder.

"You see one?" the older brother said to me.

"One what?" I replied, puzzled by the question.

"A sister," came the response.

I quickly put two and two together, and told the brother I hadn't. My response was met with, "Let us know if you see one."

A nod was enough to get me out of that situation. But I wanted to yell out, "I barely know who I am! How am I going to be a good husband?"

I was flattered to be thought of as marriage material. But I was far from ready to get married, and the "just pick one" approach seemed more like shopping than courtship. Maybe the brothers saw in me something I didn't see in myself: a suitable husband. Or perhaps I was just an unmarried brother in an environment that highly values marriage. I never asked. I didn't want to know the answer.

On the surface, I was a "good brother." I made a daily appearance at the *masjid*. I learned a lot and enjoyed the community. But the thought of courtship under the watchful eye of the community terrified me. "What if they find out I don't pray five times a day? What if someone finds out I still drink from time to time?" My fear of marriage was as much about culture shock as it was a fear that I'd be discovered to be a fraud.

I'd become an oddball in every circle I occupied. My friends and family were all Christian. Islam was foreign to the majority of people I knew. I was tasked with explaining why I fasted during one month of the year, why I was trying—and often failing—to pray five times a day, and why Muslims do or don't do whatever it was the person wanted to know about. I couldn't always answer because I didn't have all the answers.

Most of the brothers at the *masjid* were older and more conservative. I was occasionally treated to monologues about how misguided the West was. I kept my protests to myself. Everything seemed so black and white, and I was unable to articulate the beautiful shades of gray I saw every day. I was equally horrified when a brother casually talked about throwing gay people off of a cliff. I began to wonder what I'd gotten myself into and how long I could hold up.

The idea of marriage as a priority stayed with me, even when Islam didn't. I met a non-Muslim woman six months after my conversion and proposed six weeks after our first in-person meeting. I was in love and believed I had met "the one." After going through most of life feeling misunderstood, I had met someone who accepted me for who I was. We clicked immediately and found in each other a safe harbor in the rocky waters of young adult life. The news of my engagement was met with a couple of "*mashAllahs*" at the *masjid*. So ended the great "find Anthony a wife" phase.

My *iman* burned out quickly thereafter. Being with a non-Muslim woman allowed me to openly question everything I knew about organized religion without dismantling my social structure. My friends didn't care about my religion. My fiancée didn't, either. They just wanted me to be happy. Not being raised in a church and not being invested at the *masjid* allowed me to question without consequence. I drifted away from the Muslim community, spending the next five years studying different religions and philosophies about God and life. My odyssey took me from Islam, to agnosticism/atheism, back to church, back to Islam, to Buddhism, back to Islam, back to church, back to nonbelief and, finally, back to Islam again.

I kept coming back to Islam because it felt like home. I was always greeted at the *masjid* like a returning relative with an *"Assalaamu alaykum"* and a handshake. Brothers asked how I was doing and sincerely wanted to know the answer. Though I found solace in *salat*, I came back for the people.

In 2010, I divorced, adding failing to stay married to failing to stay with religion. The decision was for the best, but I felt alone in the world. What I was missing was a spiritual anchor and a greater sense of purpose. Without it, I spent the next few years in and out of relationships and empty sexual trysts.

After what seemed like an endless round of reading and research, I came back to Islam in 2013. I was praying five times a day, frequenting the *masjid*, and enjoying Islam again. I was now more open to an Islamic-style courtship. Everything else had produced dismal results. I trusted Allah. What should've been the first option was last.

Being a millennial, I signed up for a Muslim marriage site. I was hesitant to make the financial commitment to send messages on the site. The prospects in my city were few, but one sister caught my eye: "Mercy 44." Her smile was beautiful, she didn't always wear *hijab*, and her profile offered a window to her personality. Without the capability to send a full message on the site due to my irrational frugality, I sent one of those canned, "I like your profile, write back if you're interested" messages, and went on with my day, expecting nothing.

A "ping" sounded on my computer. Mercy 44 had written back! I wrestled my credit card from my wallet, punched in my information on the site, took a deep breath, and hit "send."

"Sure, feel free to tell me about yourself," her e-mail read.

I replied with my biography: Muslim man on the other side of his twenties, journalist by trade with a pair of degrees. She responded in kind. As a progressive Muslim who revels in the shades of gray, I knew to tread lightly. My pro–LGBTQ rights, pro–women's rights, separation-of-church-and-state, inclusive philosophies don't always make for easy conversation. After a couple of weeks of small talk on the marriage site, Mercy 44 and I moved our correspondence to e-mail. My hesitancy proved well founded.

We were polar opposites on nearly everything. I was a Sunni who quoted hadith on occasion; she was a Qur'an-only Muslim who believed that "Sunnis and non-Sunnis could never have full relation-ships." We agreed to disagree over the course of endless e-mails as we slung suras backing our respective positions. This wasn't a future wife, but I was intrigued and she was attractive. I've also never met a debate I didn't like, and she knew her stuff. I dropped my guard enough to begin sharing snippets of my journey. How I fell in and out of Islam, my brush with nonbelief.

She wasn't impressed. My theological adventures put me in con-tact with people of all faiths and those subscribing to none. When I mentioned that those without belief in God were also good, moral people, her disagreement turned to disgust. Things got more con-tentious when she questioned whether I was really Muslim.

"Maybe you should find some more guidance within Islam if you want to be a Muslim. Or maybe you're just a believer and not necessarily Muslim," she said.

In 99.99 percent of instances, that would've been the end of the conversation.

But it wasn't.

I was appalled. While I fancied that she saw me as a hell-bound heathen with no morals, I was still attracted to and intrigued by her boldness. I friend-zoned Mercy 44 and figured she'd eventually stop talking to me.

That didn't happen.

When we tired of arguing about all things Islam, the conversation shifted to mutual complaints about being single Muslims looking for marriage. In spite of our differences, I enjoyed the dialogue and, against all rational judgment, suggested we meet. I expected her to decline, which, I thought, would let me close this chapter and move on. To my surprise, she accepted. We agreed on bowling—probably the most halal thing a Muslim couple can do in Sin City on a Friday night.

Mercy 44 greeted me with a smile, instantly melting my defenses. I'd met women online through mainstream dating websites, but meeting a Muslim woman was another matter entirely. Sites for Muslim singles are explicitly geared toward matrimony. While what Muslims say and do are sometimes at opposite ends of the spectrum, the idea that Muslims don't "date" left me in the dark regarding Islamic courtship. We both knew the endgame. Getting there was another matter. I wasn't sure what to say or how to act. Neither was she. We looked like two teenagers at a junior high school dance, exchanging nervous laughs and cheesy grins.

The actual game of bowling wasn't as warm and fuzzy. From a woman with the screen name "Mercy 44," I received none once we hit the lanes. I hung tough through the first five frames, bowling strikes and near strikes to keep it close. As I hoisted the ball into the air to bowl my sixth, I saw a horrifying split in my jeans near my upper thigh! Frazzled by this discovery, I let the ball slip from my fingers, and it sailed into the gutter. I never regained my composure and was soundly beaten. The game was no longer of consequence. I needed to figure out how to keep from flashing the unsuspecting sister I found myself interested in getting to know.

I would later find out that Mercy 44 did notice the giant rip in my jeans. To her credit, she didn't laugh at me, which said a lot about her character. The two-hour conversation we had outside the bowling alley—ripped jeans and all—solidified my interest. We had more in common than either of us had previously imagined. We both believed Islam was best practiced through interactions with others and that appearance wasn't the sole measure of piety. We had similar tastes in music, enjoyed each other's company, and had a passion for knowledge. Our disagreements went from a source of division to an avenue for enrichment. Not seeing eye to eye on everything was okay as soon as we stopped e-mailing and started talking. She wasn't a hardliner. I wasn't a heathen. We were two people finding our way through life the best way we knew how.

What began as begrudging respect became genuine interest. As Mercy 44 and I spent more time together, we chose to focus on what we had in common, instead of our differences. Our earlier e-mails had been more about competition than conversation. Islam is important, but focusing on Qur'an over character turned minor disagreements about interpretation into a battle of wits with heavily armed combatants. We never saw eye to eye about hadith, but who cuts someone off over a disagreement about the validity of Bukhari and Muslim?

Despite setting a tentative wedding date, Mercy 44 and I never made it to the altar. Premarital counseling has a way of revealing whether one is truly ready. I wasn't. At least not at that moment. Still, our brief time together taught me a lot about compromise and not judging a book by its cover. Most important, I learned that being authentic is okay.

Instead of finding mercy at the altar, I found it in myself.

Having a safe space to share my story was liberating. I'd realized that "Anthony, the Muslim" and "Anthony, the skeptic" could coexist. I could be Muslim *and* have questions about faith. Islam felt safe again. Mercy was my red pill. She helped me escape the Matrix, the illusion I'd created that no Muslim woman would ever accept me for who I was.

Maybe I can do this marriage thing after all. Not today. But one day.

Prom, InshAllah

By Haroon Moghul

The first job I ever applied for was at McDonald's. Had my mom and dad, both doctors, discovered this, they'd have been horrified. I needed money to cover my date to the high school prom, which they weren't supposed to know about either. But, sitting in that plastic chair, testifying to my aptitude for flipping burgers, guilt wasn't the first feeling that came to mind.

I'd tried to go along. I bought into it. We didn't drink. *They* did. We didn't dance. *They* did. We didn't date. *They* did. We did not "like" girls, never mind "need" them. Somehow, it was assumed but unspoken that a spouse'd pop up, in a kind of ironclad Pakistani American Hegelianism. Thesis, antithesis, children. But there was only so long I could stand being on the sidelines.

I'd decided, come fall of my senior year, that I had to go to the prom come hell (probable) or high water (climate change). It'd be my *Ferris Bueller's Day Off*, my riding the ball in *Take Me Home Tonight*, my shot at that one unforgettable night. Even then, you see, I looked forward to life nostalgically, salivating over its reliving before it had come to pass. "Remember Haroon?" they'd say. "Who snuck out to prom?" And with who!

There are, after all, different ways of trying to live forever. Some start with an anodyne decision to cross state boundaries, like my parents did when they moved us from an old-money Massachusetts suburb to a barely postrural town. I showed up in a new school system in the middle of fifth grade; too late to make friends. Then, in sixth grade, my parents got a letter in the mail, which would change my life—by denying me one.

Not only did my mom and dad never talk to me about girls, but they also made sure that no one else did. In order to be enrolled in sex education, students needed parental permission. Every single student received it, except me. The only brown kid. The only Muslim kid. The new kid. I was assigned a project on the solar system instead of sex education and deported to the library to research it. For a doofy twelve-year-old who wore pleated pants, mismatched polos, and large, cinnamon-colored glasses, this was social homicide.

Fast-forward six years. I was a deeply superficial upperclass-man—for someone so stunningly awkward, I was convinced I had a shot with the school's hottest girls. But I wasn't *just* interested in them for their bodies. I really wanted someone to hold hands with. Someone to see the world and share it with. Someone to make sure I'd never be alone again. Because I was many things: narcissistic (no one should leave me) and despondent (everyone will one day).

By my senior year, the battle of immigrant *Geist* versus female corporeality had been decided. Not only did I want to go to prom, I wanted a date to it. She turned out to be a sophomore named Carla, who first came to my attention one day late in March. My good friend Jeremy and I were walking the senior hallway after school when Carla stepped out of a classroom she shouldn't have been in. She stopped and looked both ways. She waved hello to him—she didn't know me—and walked ahead of us.

Even Jeremy, ever the embodiment of propriety (and piety), muttered an "Oh, my goodness" before he noticed my staring and suggested I stop. This I liked Jeremy for: he treated religion reli-giously. A man of God, but one who danced and dated, and so he threw me for a loop. When I admitted to Jeremy I was smitten by Carla's Italian genes, her stonewashed jeans, and her striped green tank top, he swore to help me make the leap from fantasy to reality.

On a Wednesday in early April, I was taken from school to at-tend *Eid* prayers at the closest mosque, some forty miles north, where the Muslim part of me was all but born and bred. As usual, we had to wake up uncomfortably early to not get stuck in the un-snowplowed outré-mer of the Islamic center's parking lot. Also, you wanted a short walk from the car to the building so you didn't freeze to death. Our obstinate Punjabi-ness demanded we wear *shalwar kameez*, no matter its inappropriateness for the weather.

If *Eid* was one thing growing up, it was boring. Among the few upsides, we got some money—mine, it should be noted, helped pay for Carla's corsage. Which meant she said yes. Let me tell you how.

I was home from *Eid* prayers by late afternoon, and called Jeremy to find out what I'd missed in school. As if, as a senior, I really cared. Turned out I'd missed only everything. During eighth-period English, Carla had stopped by our class. She had a message for her older sister, a senior like us.

To call me crestfallen would be dishonest. I was shattered. Carla, with the wavy hair, which smelled like heaven, underneath which rivers flow? Carla, with the mesmerizingly sapphire eyes?

"Did she look hot like she always does?" I asked.

Jeremy answered elliptically. "You should hurry up and ask her before someone else does."

How exactly should I do that?

I'd never talked to her, never acknowledged her, never, so far as I could tell, been noticed by her. But so badly did I want to that I tossed social anxiety aside and decided to ask out one of my Abrahamic coreligionists the day after celebrating his near-sacrifice of his son. It should've been easy enough. Because, for one thing, her sister had already told her of my interest.

Carla's locker was right outside our AP biology classroom, which is where I'd make the ask, except I lost my nerve at the last minute and sought refuge in that same classroom, until her cousin Bradley showed up with a huge grin on his face. "Did you do it?" he asked, entirely rhetorically until he saw my expression.

"Umm, no."

"What the hell is wrong with you?" He may or may not have said that. Because Bradley had other ways of communicating. Upset with my spinelessness, Bradley punched me. To add insult to social injury, he shoved me out the door. This meant I came into Carla's line of sight by flying out of a classroom and halfway across the hall. I tried not to think about how this looked. Her friends scattered at the sudden sight of me, because they knew what I was there for.

"Hey, Carla . . ."

She turned to give me her full attention. This was not helpful.

"I was wondering if you—"

"Yes?"

"Would, uh, want to go to the prom?" I'm really not sure if I included the "with me"; I may have simply inquired into her interest in the function generally.

"Sure, I'd love to."

Then she slammed her locker shut and said she had to get to class.

I like to think I stood there like a Punjabi Peter Parker, when he first becomes aware of his super spidery powers. I felt a new man— taller, better, braver, and a cooler shade of brown. High on myself, I spun around and nearly ran over Mrs. D., my AP biology teacher. Who'd been behind me during the entire exchange.

She practically gave me a black-power salute: "Good work, Haroon!"

I was mortified. "You saw that?"

By the end of that day, the whole science department had congratulated me. I should, in honor of this alliance, apologize for scoring a 2 on the actual AP exam. More important things were unfolding.

My parents left town a few weekends later; Carla and I talked on the phone and agreed we were "dating." You might at this point think me possessed of incredible memory. Rather, it's that I wrote volumes of poetry, as every bookish kid my age would; they are my photographs. They recorded, mostly, what I didn't do. Except this time I did.

For our first date, I'd gone all the way to Westfield, which had the closest Friendly's. Her father told her, by which he meant me, not to be late, but we were. We talked over frothy chocolate milkshakes. About what, I don't know. Didn't care.

Our two months together were my AP in assimilation. How do dates work? (Ask friends.) Am I allowed to check her out because she's my girlfriend? (Answer didn't matter.) Holy crap, she's going out with me. (Holy crap, she's going out with me.) The whole not-touching thing didn't last either. Late one Saturday night in May I decided to kiss her.

We pulled up to her house and I walked her to the side door, under the porch, one of those halfhearted basements, part underground and part above. (I sympathized with this bipolarity.) When she turned to face me, ostensibly to say goodnight, I stared stupidly into her eyes until she asked, "Is everything okay?"

"I wanted to kiss you."

She went with it. Carla approached me slowly, gingerly, and when she got close enough, closed her eyes and reached up toward me, tilting her head ever so slightly. I was kissed. Nothing I'd read prepared me for that feeling—pure joy, a wave displacing everything else inside of me. Rapture had come to lift me up and away. I kissed her back, and a second later it was over. She smiled and disappeared into her house.

Did she know I'd never kissed a girl before?

And then, a week or two later, my parents found out. My mom called me downstairs first thing in the morning. She stood on one side of the kitchen and my father on the other. Trying to play it cool, I focused on breakfast. My mother glanced at my father.

This was his cue. "Why did you have a girl in your car yesterday?"

Someone in the Muslim community—the local *mukhabarat*—had snitched on me.

I shrugged. "She needed a ride home."

They stared into me. Hard. They could tell I was guilty of something. But what? Since offering a girl a ride home was already a moral trespass, maybe that and that alone was the worst of my deeds, the source of the guilt in my eyes. I folded an Eggo in half and shoved most of it into my mouth, washing it down with a glass of chocolate milk. "It was nothing."

Though it most certainly was not. It was the most important thing ever to happen to me. But that was a close call, which meant I'd have to outsmart the local morality police. I started my own Arab Spring. My actions had to be kept hidden, though at great cost to posterity. For example: friends were asked to submit prophecies for the graduating seniors' yearbook; Jeremy thought it'd be a riot to submit "Haroon dates a supermodel."

Which meant when my parents asked me about yearbook photos—another letter in the mail—I had to move preemptively. "Yearbooks are stupid," I said, doing my best impression of a jaded teenager, permanently bored out of his mind. "I'm not going to have my picture taken for that crap."

So they never asked for my yearbook, and never found even the flimsiest evidence of my double life. The yearbook editors were proactive; they assumed I'd forgotten to submit a proper photograph, and helpfully found the worst possible picture of me, slapping it above my name, such that any future reader would wonder what kind of washed-out supermodel would date that man. It was too late, though, to try to erase myself from history: Months before, I'd submitted a quote. Pearl Jam. These were the years when we were too new to understand ourselves. We needed music to explain us to us. "All that is sacred comes from youth."

McDonald's never called back, so I found another job: helping my fellow students polish off their assignments. Technically I did not graduate high school once but several times.

I'd walk past Carla every morning; I *needed* to see her. Touch her. "To breathe. To feel. To know I'm alive." Tool. I was years away from understanding my depression, years further from learning what to do with it. But I knew what Carla did, how she made me feel. Before her, what I thought was numbness was really a desperate, terrifying loneliness.

My friends teased me for not yet making out with her; I, too, wondered why I held back. Her friend Samantha sprang a pool party on us at the end of May, which I knew I had to attend—I'd make my move then and there. But of course her house had to be next door to that of our *masjid* president, which meant he might see my car. A huge risk to take two weeks before prom—but this new Haroon loved the edge.

Not enough, however, to drive his car over it. I asked my friend Jacob to be my ride. And, of course, on the way over, his nose started bleeding so badly that he all but ran his station wagon aground on someone's lawn, opened his door, and nearly tripped into the grass. Then he sprinted to the closest tree, whose leaves were repurposed as napkins.

We met the homeowner, who had real napkins too, which she shared after we explained why a plurality of our town's young Semites were frolicking around her favorite tree. This unfathomable omen aside, I ended up that night exactly where I'd wanted to: on Samantha's pool deck. With Carla. But for the first time, things did not go my way. And they would keep on not going my way from then on.

Blind children learn how to walk without seeing anyone else do so—it's deep instinct, buried inside them, and just needs to find the right time and place. I felt myself overcome with desire, but (and this was the best part) I could sense, with some radar I did not know I had (but would never again neglect), that Carla wanted the same thing. Opposite ends of a magnet. I knew what to do and for the first time how to. Fusion releases more energy than fission.

But we put more energy in than we got out. Her mom pulled up much earlier than expected. I walked Carla to her car, dejected, but as she made her way to the door, she offered me her hand in apology. My skinny fingers squeezed inside her smaller, softer, subtler hand. There was so much in that grasp, and I feared I'd spend my life trying only to return to that squeeze. Because there were no more such nights.

I led my parents to believe that on *the* Friday night, the first week of June, I'd sleep over a (Muslim) friend's house in Massachusetts; his (Muslim) mom covered for me. After school, I crossed state lines, where I showered and shaved, and then returned to our hometown just in time for events to be set in motion.

Jacob's neighbors were on vacation, so I parked my hulking beige and brown SUV not merely in their backyard, but under their deck. Just in case my parents wandered up a driveway many streets away from their own and decided to look around. Then I went to Jacob's house and threw caution to the wind, because I had to have some kind of memory of this: photographs.

Back then, you had to wait weeks for them to develop. You actually got to live in the moment, as opposed to looking at yourself living it a few seconds later, which meant the moment lasted considerably longer than a moment. The six of us, me, Jacob, Jeremy, and our dates—looked damn good, I must say. I have no other pictures of Carla. Just the smiles we wore for the camera, belying what was around the corner. I never got to thank her, though.

See, she held back on what she wanted, and gave me my night. Many students congratulated me, amazed I'd made it. Amazed I'd wanted to—everyone's belief system appreciates validation. And I wanted theirs. Maybe so that one day I wouldn't need it. We had steak and pounding music. Then Carla and I slow-danced to Sarah McLachlan's "Adia," which to this day I cannot listen to without getting goose bumps.

Carla was in my arms, like she'd been only a few times before in the past months (once after a flute solo in a school concert, once on the occasion of her communion). I couldn't shake the thought: why was God sending me an Islamic meme here, of all places? "We are born innocent," McLachlan sings. And Satan asked Adam, "Shall I lead you to a Tree, and to a Kingdom that never decays?"

Time stopped for me in that slow dance; I felt poetry flow through me. I've learned, in the years since, to pull over whenever an idea enters my mind. Published essays have been typed at New Jersey rest stops, or in the Istanbul airport, where there is no seating.

"Believe me, Adia. We are still innocent." I was convinced I still was. We all were. No matter where I was or who I was touching. We can do the wrong thing for the right reasons. It depends on whether you think gray is still close to God. Adam and Eve both ate from the tree, but they repented. They were forgiven. But they stuck together. That is the point of innocence lost. It reclaims itself when it restores itself.

I was a seventeen-year-old who wanted more than anything in the world to belong. The flared jeans, the metal necklaces, the occasional bracelets: the tribal markers of an aspiring snowboarder were meant to validate me by announcing that I was other than me. Sticking out to fit in. But even these emblems couldn't tell you how badly I'd wanted this cheerleader.

We can want what others want and still want it for ourselves. Sometimes we're unable to point to where our desires begin and others' end. After prom we might have stopped at Friendly's, but Carla wanted nothing to do with me. The next afternoon, alone in an empty bedroom in someone else's house in Massachusetts, half an hour from home, Carla turned to AOL Instant Messenger to shock and awe me: We should break up, she suggested.

Of course, I typed. I lied. My parents drove me to New York that night, to see family, but I sat broken in the backseat—they must have known something was wrong. But I could not tell them how my end run around them had failed because I was, in the end, them. We never moved beyond that kiss; I'd been more Catholic than the Catholic girl. This is human nature, or at least my fragment of *fitra*, what's left of the Adam in you after Satan's through. To me, dating was no different than marrying. Terminology was technicality.

I was shattered like I couldn't believe. My religion says a man should not be alone with a woman. But somebody should have told me a man should not feel so alone that being with a woman is the only way he can feel life is worth living.

If every person has one great test, then mine was—and may still be—parting. I could deal with death. If I was a good Muslim (which I'm not), I believed I'd see the people I cared about down the line. We're going to live on, forever and ever, Oasis sang. God would add: So will everyone else. But I couldn't accept that God would let lives intersect, get entangled, and then be yanked apart. How can you live forever and be parted forever?

The further you let a person into your soul, the longer it'll take her to leave. The first time I saw Carla, she was walking away from me. I couldn't have guessed then how much it would hurt to give anyone anything of my heart, so I'd naively given all of mine. My college friends, who met me a few months later, can tell you it took me a year to get over a girl I dated for less than two months.

The idea of Carla preceded her, and survived long after her. Her smile, her lightness, her kindness, all of them a bond she provided to a universe I otherwise felt misplaced by. But what I missed most of all, for months on end: her hand. From the first time she offered it to me, at a roller-skating rink (a dance remix of Celine Dion's unavoidable "My Heart Will Go On" was playing), to the last, when we left the dance floor and I escorted her to our table.

"It may be you hate a thing and it is good for you." That would be God. Beyond my desire for Carla was an awesome loneliness, a feeling of living in a nothing-place only briefly interrupted. From time to time, this emptiness made the world stark and beautiful, but most of the time it haunted and pursued me. After enough years had passed and enough hurt accumulated, I began to pursue the emptiness instead. Something came from nothing: "With every difficulty there's relief." Him again. It could be that this is me, or all of us. We stumble onto God in the blanks, the places you live in but don't belong to, if only to be taught this hell of a mercy: no one belongs here.

Sabr: In Sickness and in Health

The Promise

By Alan Howard

I first met Joan in 1992 in New York, a city I had not planned on visiting, at a conference I had been skeptical about attending. I had just completed my first year in college and was still getting my bearings. Traveling to the United Nations headquarters for a collegiate conference on international crisis resolution was not something I wanted to do.

Nor were love and romance on my mind. I was a shy, geeky nineteen-year-old. Although a closet romantic, talking or interacting with women was not my forte. As I stood near the doors of the cavernous conference room surveying the eager college students within, my eyes lit upon a petite, beautiful Asian woman. I then did something I had never done before: I walked straight across the room and introduced myself. I've often wondered why I did this, since it was so uncharacteristic of me. I have no answers except that it was meant to happen.

Joan was funny and laughed a lot. She had a way of evaluating a situation in a matter of seconds, a quick intelligence and a focused intensity that allowed her to plot a course of action immediately. The rest of the conference is a blur in my memory. We attended sessions but spent the entire time passing notes back and forth discussing politics, family, our dreams, and everything in between. No subject was left untouched, and yet not a word passed our lips.

On the last evening, we sat down in a quiet hallway to talk face to face.

"What is that long scar on your neck?" I asked innocently, reaching out to brush it gently.

She stiffened and immediately turned away from me. Her hand instinctively moved to rub it, as if she'd just remembered it was there. She sighed, silent for a few seconds. "It's from a surgery. I have cancer."

Boom! Just like that, she introduced me to a terrifying part of her world.

Joan stared at me, curious to see my reaction, whatever her fears may have been. She seemed to be daring me: would I risk being interested in someone who was sick?

"Do you let it stop you from doing what you want with your life?" I asked.

And then, as if my first question wasn't forward enough, I added, "The cancer affects you, but it doesn't define you. What do you plan to do with your life?"

Years later, Joan told me that it was that statement that led her to believe that I was the person she wanted to be with for the rest of her life.

After the conference, Joan returned to California and I returned to South Carolina, where I was attending college. A continent separated us but we managed to talk often. We came from very different backgrounds. I was born and raised in South Carolina. The Deep South is a land of warm ocean currents, Spanish moss, history-filled towns, bad politics, and racial divisions. She was born to Filipino immigrants in San Francisco and raised in California. We found we complemented each other.

The first time I called Joan was awkward. She told me later she'd never expected to hear from me again. I took to calling every Tuesday evening to check on her and to talk. Over time our calls turned into hours-long conversations. She said she knew she loved me when she was late one Tuesday and ran as fast as she could to get to the phone before I called. I knew I loved her almost in the same instant that I saw her in that crowded conference room. I'd never felt that way about someone. Even then, like a magnet she drew me in.

A year later, I asked her father's permission to marry her. Three months later, she moved cross-country and we married at my local mosque—nothing fancy, just a few dozen friends and my parents. I had converted to Islam during my first year of college after spending a long time battling personal demons and studying several religions. Joan converted in her own time three years later. We had little in terms of material wealth as I was still finishing up at the university, but we took trips together, talked about everything in our lives, and explored the South. We were unbelievably happy, going on long walks and holding hands, oblivious to anyone else. Exploring new foods or destinations together instead of individually was wonderful, like discovering a secret garden only we knew about.

When we met, Joan's cancer was in remission. We didn't want to think that it would resurface, interrupting our dreams as individuals and as a family. We moved to California for a year. We had a second marriage ceremony in Oakland, where she had attended college, so that her family could attend this time. We spent many fun weeks exploring San Francisco and Berkeley, but ultimately decided that California was too expensive.

We settled in Atlanta in 1997 and she and I began our careers in finance and IT, respectively. Having a major international airport in Atlanta allowed us to travel in Europe, Asia, and Africa. Each new destination expanded our knowledge of each other and of other people and cultures. We began talking about starting a family, although we weren't initially sure if Joan could have children, given her medical history.

Our "good" years were filled with love and lovemaking, joy and fun, travel and discovery. And, finally, the blessed birth of our son, Jibril, in 2000. Joan embraced motherhood. She loved to put Jibril in a wagon and run around the yard with him, while he screamed happily. She would take him hiking in the forests and watch his face fill with wonder when holding a tree frog or touching a mushroom.

In 2005, the cancer came back. Joan was working on her PhD in economics at Georgia State University. Jibril was five years old—too young to understand.

For the next eight years, our marriage was filled with radiation and chemotherapy treatments, thirteen surgeries, and countless visits to specialists. With every new surgery and treatment, I lost another piece of my beautiful wife.

Our small family adjusted as well as we could to each new development. There were chemotherapy treatments that caused Joan incontinence or extreme nausea; surgeries that meant months of recovery; brain tumors that led to an inability to use her left hand; pelvic damage that caused a pronounced limp on her right side; and fluid that built up in her lungs and forced her to be on oxygen all the time. It was overwhelming. But Joan transformed into a mighty warrior, fighting for her life every second of every day. I, on the other hand, hated it. I hated what it did to her. I hated what it made her become and hated that the cancer robbed my son and me of her active presence in our lives.

Joan's faith shaped her response to everything—good or bad—that happened. She believed that God tests each of us over the course of our lives with challenges. These are not to prove anything to God, who is infinite and knows the outcome, but, rather, to prove to ourselves what we are capable of as humans. For Joan there were no "Why me?" moments. She had *sabr*, an Arabic word that encompasses both patience and perseverance. Anyone can be patient, but to have patience in the face of hardship requires *sabr*.

Unlike my wife, I became very angry with God when she got sick. I stopped practicing my faith for a full year—no prayer, no reflection, nothing. Looking back, I don't believe that I lost my faith so much as I unconsciously thought I was punishing Allah by refusing to worship Him. But the sicker Joan became, the more I was drawn back to Allah and the need to pray for her—for her recovery, for the strength to care for her, and, finally, weeping uncontrollably, for her release from pain and suffering.

Through Joan's ordeal, I learned to accept that there are things that happen in this world that I do not understand and cannot control, but must face with *sabr* anyway. Joan's embodiment of Islam taught me how to understand and survive the tests I have been given in life, in order to grow and change and become more beautiful. The Qur'an states, "And, behold, with every hardship comes ease: verily, with every hardship comes ease!" (Sura ash-Sharh [The Opening-Up of the Heart], 94: 5–6.) My wife's test in this life was cancer; it changed her and made her strong. My test was to take care of her, to never turn away. It was my duty to stand by her, but it was also my love. It was the core of my humanity.

After eight years of suffering, my wife of eighteen years decided to stop treatment in order to spend her last days here on this earth with dignity. Joan died in December 2012. She was only forty-one years old.

Now that Joan is gone, many friends have asked me: If I'd known the struggles to come, the pain, the horror, and the heartache of watching her live and die, would I have still stepped forward into our relationship? The answer is a resounding YES. I would do it all again—the postsurgical therapies, cleaning up her vomit after chemotherapy treatments, bathing her when she could no longer bathe herself, carrying her tenderly up and down the stairs of our home when her energy was depleted, helping to dress her—because to do so would mean that she was alive and still with us.

Joan told me once that while she hated what the cancer had done to her body, she would not be who she was without having endured it. Cancer taught her how to face death without fear; it taught her what she was capable of handling. Without the cancer she may have grown old, but perhaps would not have been as strong. Facing death showed her that she did not have time to waste. She even defined her approaching demise as simply, "Needing some time to rest."

"I will love you forever," I promised my wife repeatedly during our eighteen years together. Only she and I know what that truly means. Joan loved me with her constant encouragement to live up to my full potential. Life without her is frightening, but also holds limitless possibilities because of what I learned from her. Continuing to love her after she is gone means doing something new or different every day, continually discovering so that I never stop growing.

In my devastation, as I mourn the passing of my wife, our marriage, and the most beautiful experiences of my life, I still wake up every day living this promise to her: I will never stop growing. God bless you, *habibti.*

Fertile Ground

By Khizer Husain

We are in a bright corner office. Outside is the Baltimore skyline. Trees like torches. The air is crisp. We are seated across from Dr. Zacur, who is sketching a portrait on graph paper. Suddenly, he looks up.

"Your ovaries have no eggs."

I snap out of my daydream. Zuleqa is slumped in her chair. "I never say that someone has no chance of conceiving, but . . ." His voice trails off. The portrait of Zuleqa's condition in his hands is titled "Idiopathic."

He continues, "We could take a donor egg." He looks at Zuleqa. "Do you have a sister?"

Zuleqa nods. I am no Islamic scholar, but I'm pretty sure that my gametes and those of my sister-in-law should not mix. Idiopathic sounds more idiotic and pathetic by the minute.

I am numb and speechless. This was not part of the plan. I stare at Zacur's bowtie. The room suddenly feels like a sauna. Did Zacur just call my wife defective? Can we crack open a window in here? I can't breathe!

I want to blame Zacur, but it's tough to hate a man like him. He's a Norman Rockwellian doctor who probably used to make house calls early in his practice. But now I wish that he'd step out of the room. We need privacy. I know Zuleqa needs a hug. I've learned in our six years of marriage that hugs are the currency of love, the strongest refuge during storms. Hugs can articulate what words can't—I am here for you, *jaanu*. We'll get through this, *inshAllah*.

Reproductive endocrinologists are optimists. There's always some possibility for fertility. Our fertility probability is 10 percent. Does that mean we have to try ten times harder to conceive? Is it all moot if there are no eggs? How does he know there are no eggs? Ultrasounds look like WWII–era technology for finding German U-boats. What about my side of the equation: are there legions of healthy swimmers, or a sorry mess incapable of doing the job?

Zacur stands, signaling that our appointment is at an end. He relates a story of a young patient who had the same diagnosis, primary ovarian insufficiency (POI). He thought she had no chance of conceiving, but she came back twenty years later with a baby in her arms. "That's why I vowed to tell my patients there is hope—but don't bet the farm on it." In other words, we might be able to get that senior citizen discount at diapers.com.

I have a lot of questions I cannot articulate. Zuleqa is uncharacteristically quiet. Anyway, our time is over. Another anxious couple waits. I force a smile their way as we make our way out. *Good luck—I hope Zacur sketches a happier graph paper portrait for you.*

Zuleqa and I courted for about ten hours over ten days in the spring of 1999 in Hyderabad. She was starting med school. I was on spring break from grad school in London.

"Farawla. Doesn't it sound like a perfect name for a girl?" I offered over strawberry ice cream on our first date at Softy World.

"Of course!" Zuleqa held back a laugh.

I told her about the epiphany I had while studying in Cairo a couple of years earlier—that the Arabic word for strawberry would be the perfect nickname for my first-born daughter. It just sounded right: F-R-W-LA. Delicate, warm, earthy. Based on my brothers' track records, I was destined to have a daughter. The "Y" guys were just too bashful.

We married the following year. We never talked directly about whether we would have children. As with most Muslim couples we knew, having kids was a question of when, not if. We each had three siblings, and parents who came from colossal families. Yet our maternal and paternal clocks didn't dictate our lives. We did not "ooh" and "aah" at the mere sight of babies or have an urge to hold them at dinner parties. Still, the POI diagnosis caught us flat-footed because we'd never *not* thought of having children. Chapters in our lives that we'd set aside for kids now needed to be replaced. But with what?

The U.S. immigration process forced us to live apart the first year of our marriage: I in Illinois, Zuleqa in Hyderabad. We e-mailed and called but when my brothers announced their intention to go on hajj, I climbed aboard. Zuleqa's parents were expats living in Makkah, so coordinating a hajj rendezvous was straightforward. The "hajj-y-moon" was spectacular—spiritually and otherwise. A month later, I got a call from Zuleqa.

In a meek voice: "Jaan, I missed my period." There was a pause. "Hello? Did you hear me?"

I cleared my throat. "Um, say that again."

"You heard me." She sounded giddy.

"Not really. Reception's bad. Static-y."

"*Mera paun bhari hai.*"

"Your foot is weighty?" I tried to decipher the Urdu idiom.

"Khizer . . . I'm pregnant!"

My heart started racing. Good God. Terrific news—I think. We had less than two grand in the bank and neither of us had a job. Gulp.

"*Mubarak!* This is fantastic. *Alhamdulillah.*" I paused. Breathed. I heard a muffled giggle.

Knowing Zuleqa's mischievous streak, I suggested, "Why don't you break the good news to Ammi? She'll want to hear it directly from you. Here . . ."

"No! Wait!"

"What's the matter?"

"Nothing."

"Okay. Ammi, Zuleqa has a very important announcement."

"Ah . . . jheesh. Khizer—April Fool's?"

I sighed, relieved. "You *conceived* a fine ruse, madam."

In the months following the diagnosis, we remember those innocent exchanges. April Fool's smacks more of April irony and *farawla*
of some forbidden fruit. So, we aren't going to have kids. Not a big
deal, right? There are tons of infertile people. A few months prior to
our diagnosis a cousin had revealed his. After years of trying IVF,
he and his wife were putting it on hold. The emotional highs and
lows were taking a toll.

Not having kids is probably a good thing, I rationalize—the
planet is overcrowded and the Qur'an says God will test you with
wealth and children.

Wealth and children are an adornment of this world's life:
but good deeds, the fruit whereof endures forever, are of far
greater merit in thy Sustainer's sight, and a far better source
of hope. (Sura al-Kahf [The Cave], 18:46)

Zuleqa and I recite the first few words like they're a *tasbih*—no
money, no kids, no problem. One less thing to be tested with. We're
God-seeking people: if God does not want us to have kids, then we
should be fine with not having kids.

But to have peace with this was not so easy.

"Would you have married me if you'd known about the diagnosis?"
Zuleqa asked casually as I was chopping onions.

"*Bilkul*," I said reflexively. I'd actually never thought about it.

"Why would you?" she pressed.

"Because I loooovvvvve you," I crooned. Zuleqa had the "I'm
serious" look. I went to hug her but she dodged. Not this time.

"Look, I'm not crushed that we will probably not have kids," I explained. "But I would be devastated if I did not have you."

I stared into her eyes. She opened up for a hug. I squeezed hard. Rivers ran down our faces. I blamed it on the onions.

Over the next few months, we talk less about the diagnosis. Other things in life come to the fore. Drama at work. The funeral of a close family friend. The Cherry Blossom Festival. We get into the routine of Zuleqa's new assortment of pills and patches. It's tough enough for a twentysomething to keep on regimen. I have no idea how seniors do it. The next time I pick up her meds at the pharmacy, I get a weekly pill dispenser. It's purple. When I give it to her, Zuleqa smiles with her eyes.

"Let's explore adoption," I suggest one evening. It's been a year since our visit with Zacur. Adoption is a tough topic, partly because it implies "giving up" on having biological kids and partly because I know that "Muslims don't adopt." Zuleqa had related the practice of "adoption" in the old country, where people give their own children to those in the family who can't have kids. Years later a teenage girl realizes that the people she had believed to be her parents are actually her biological aunt and uncle. Recipe for resentment, if you ask me.

We attend the Freddie Mac Foundation Adoption Expo in Washington, DC. It's a happy carnival of smiling faces of children and eager couples. Everyone is incredibly nice; I feel like I did when I attended Apostolic service as a junior high schooler in Iowa with my good friend Curt and his family. Here is the thing—this time around, I want to be converted. I know that adoption can be a great solution, which allows love to flourish. Plus, we know that adoption among American Muslims is needed. Some kid in a bad situation will help us to complete our family. But front and center in my mind is a nagging question: which one of us—Zuleqa or me—will not be able to hug our postpubescent adopted child? *Mahrameyat*—the concept that you can be physically close to those of the opposite gender only if they are related through blood and marriage—makes adoption unpalatable. I know it's small in the grand scheme of things, but it's a pretty big deal to us.

Were we being too "*fiqh-y*"? Islam prescribes emphatic support for orphans.

> *They will ask thee as to what they should spend on others. Say: "Whatever of your wealth you spend shall (first) be for your parents, and for the near of kin, and the orphans, and the needy, and the wayfarer; and whatever good you do, verily, God has full knowledge thereof. (Sura al-Baqara [The Cow], 2:215)*

Yet Islam advises against "Western" adoption and supports foster parenting instead—love the child, but they should know their biological lineage and keep their birth family name. There should be no confusion about their heritage so that they maintain their own identity. Perhaps we can revisit this option in the future. Foster parenting seems like temporary parenting and, like temporary marriage, doesn't seem to sit right. We don't know any foster parents in our community; we don't have the courage to be pioneers.

"Khizer, I found this Muslim fertility doctor who practices in the metro area. We should see her. Get a Muslim perspective." Zuleqa spent random evenings on the Internet searching for insight into her rare condition. I was supportive of a second opinion.

I can't get time off work, so Zuleqa flies solo. Not a good idea. Dr. Abbasi turns out to be everything we don't want in a doctor. Listening is not her forte. She plows over Zuleqa's sentences with an "I've heard these stories a million times." Her solution is adamantly pro–egg donation.

Zuleqa asks, "What does Islamic bioethics—"

Abbasi barks, "Look, Zuleqa. I have so many Muslim patients. Do you want to have children or not?"

This was the nadir of the infertility episode. POI is tough—a life sentence of hormone replacement therapy just to be as normal as possible. Falling off the regimen can increase the risk of certain cancers. Zuleqa thought that a Muslim specialist would be an asset, someone who understood our needs and could guide us in this uncharted journey. Abbasi turned out to be a bully. We felt betrayed by one of our own, and that stung.

Abbasi might have found it unremarkable for some donor egg to hook up with my sperm and for that embryo to be transplanted into my wife's womb, but we had tons of questions. For this to work within *Shia fiqh*, would I need to first marry the donor? I don't want to be the first bigamist in my family, even if it's for a few hours. If the baby is male, would breastfeeding him be sufficient to make him *mahram* to Zuleqa? And how would we explain this to our child? "Well *munnu*, half your genes come from this nice lady your mom and I met at the egg bank. So, yes, you have two moms, but not in the same way as Jenny at school . . ."

Our families are supportive. Faith is strong among the parents, and no one freaks out about POI. They do introduce us to a plethora of *duas* and special *namaaz* for having children. I find the *ayah* involving Prophet Zakaria to be a tongue twister, but it is powerful:

> *AND [thus did We deliver] Zakaria when he cried out unto his Sustainer: "O my Sustainer! Leave me not childless! But [even if Thou grant me no bodily heir, I know that] Thou wilt remain when all else has ceased to be!" (Sura al-Ambiyaa [The Prophets], 21:89)*

Zuleqa is more diligent in these prayers than I am. I am a bit confused theologically: are we supposed to pray hard to miraculously have kids, accept the test of being childless, or both? I want to close the fecundity chapter and move on—thankful and childless.

No to egg donors, no to adoption or foster parenting. If kids happen, great. If not, no problem.

Much more difficult is keeping at bay *masjid* aunties who have a compulsion to know about everyone's marital and reproductive lives.

"*Beta*, how many years you have been married. When will you give us the good news?"

Zuleqa has an incredible gift for understanding and empathizing with these aunties. Having grown up in India definitely helps. She waves off these probes with a "Just keep us in your *duas*, aunty," or a "You'll be the first to know." I lack this finesse. In fact, I'm sure that I would have caused many embarrassing *masjid* incidents had it not been for the high perimeter fence surrounding the sisters' section and the constant din of wailing kids drowning out the Fertility Inquisition.

I wonder if the prophets who had trouble having kids faced the same type of aunty full-court fertility press in their time? Can you picture Prophet Ibrahim consoling Sarah after some aunty goes on about having fourteen kids before she was thirty? Maybe Prophet Zakaria trying for decades to convince a gang of uncles that he is totally fine not having children. "I really don't need to continue my family line . . . aren't we all children of Ibrahim?" he'd remind them.

What does annoy Zuleqa are the odder fertility rituals that well-wishers from the old country prescribe. "Boil these twigs and bark and drink the potion every Friday—before *fajr*." "Tie this string around your midsection and leave it there for forty days." "Buy this maryam herbal plant in the holy city of Makkah and soak it in water and leave it by your bedside every night until you conceive, become pregnant, and go into labor." We amass a community apothecary that she wants to throw out. I don't have the heart to tell these friends and relatives that we won't be needing their ancient wisdom.

Three years into the diagnosis, Zuleqa looks up from her computer screen. "*Jaanu*, check this out!" The National Institutes of Health was conducting a study on individuals with POI. Zuleqa needed a real second opinion and the NIH was forty-five minutes away in Bethesda. Zuleqa would need to send her medical records to see if she could join the study to develop treatments to restore fertility and to determine the ideal form of hormone replacement. In May 2009, Zuleqa received the thick package from the NIH, with her appointment calendar and details for her four days onsite.

In July, I helped Zuleqa get situated in her semiprivate room at the NIH hospital: "You'll have a great time at POI Camp! See you on Family Night on Wednesday." She was anxious. I kissed her forehead and said, "*Khuda hafiz.*"

Each night, I received updates. "In our Zacur and Abbasi visits the conversation was so clinical, so focused on my hormone levels," Zuleqa said. "It was nice to have a health professional allow me to speak about POI in the larger picture of what makes me happy in life."

I thought about those instances that bring out the best in Zuleqa—spontaneous picnics, hosting a *sham-e-ghazal*, organizing scavenger hunts at family reunions. We have built a life creating community that transcends faith, family, or ethnic lines. Zuleqa is fun, a ball of energy. POI does not define her, nor does infertility.

The next day, I went for the group session with Dr. Lawrence, the lead investigator of the study. He was engaging, funny, realistic, and had time for questions. When Zuleqa and I stepped out of the hospital to head home, the summer air felt good. Zuleqa was beaming.

What does it mean to be childless for us?

"I am perfectly happy helping to rear my nieces and nephews," says my incredible wife.

I completely agree.

We had dinner with my cousin who tried IVF and is also childless. He said the same thing. He has powerful relationships with his siblings' kids, in which he can hang out with them, guide them, and scold them. In essence, he is reviving an Indian tradition that has faded away amid the nuclear families and individualism in the U.S.

I see us as "coach-parents"—we know enough of the theory of parenting from our own observations to offer perspective. Send them to our place for winter break. We'll give them an insider's tour of Washington. Confused about college options? We can provide some guidance—including how to spot the FBI in your MSA. Challenged by potty training? We have some novel approaches you might fancy, depending on your risk tolerance.

We also have the capacity and thirst to create a vibrant extended family. Zuleqa and I are helping to plan a mega family reunion of three hundred people over three days. Channeling our energy gives us purpose and meaning.

What's more, our experience has taught us that as a community, we need to do a better job of creating safe spaces for individuals and couples to talk about uncomfortable issues without triggering an avalanche of criticism and/or advice. Sometimes what is needed is not a parent but a coach—to provide perspective without judgment, support without pity, help without strings attached. Allah says in the Qur'an that you will be tested in this life by what you have been given and what you have not been given. We have been given POI, which liberates us to take unique roles in the family and in our community.

The ground is fertile for action.

On Guard

By Stephen Leeper

The first time I met Aliyah, in 2011, we smiled at each other, guarded. The imam had just reminded us during *Jumma* to have *taqwa*, to be on guard. Neither of us needed that reminder though: we had already mastered it. Sister Elizabeth introduced us and stood off to the side, watching us build our invisible fortresses. Later, I tweeted, "Met a beautiful Muslima today." I was terrified at the prospect of getting to know her, but I wanted nothing more.

It was the second year after I'd moved from North Carolina to California. I had moved to escape boredom and childhood memories, leaving Ashley, my beautiful non-Muslim girlfriend, behind. We had been a couple for a few months, but had known each other for two years. She said she would leave with me "just like that"—she didn't have to see a five-year plan or a five-digit number in my bank account. My promise was all she needed. I left North Carolina in September 2009 and started making plans for our future. By January, she had left me for her white ex-boyfriend, a blow to the Original Blackman's ego, a carryover sentiment from my Stephen X days.

The next year was one of grief and sorrow filled with bitter, desperate crying when I got up in the morning, in my car between meetings, and in bed at night. Unlike with the Prophet, neither my uncle nor my wife had died, but my hope had, and I grieved. When I met Aliyah the following autumn, I had healed a great deal but was fucking terrified of opening up again.

A few weeks later, Sister Elizabeth invited Aliyah to a community meeting I'd organized at the San Francisco Muslim Community Center. I was a faith-based community organizer with the San

Francisco Organizing Project (SFOP) at the time, and relationship building was part of my job description. The meeting's focus was on developing transformational relationships as the basis of powerful organization for change. My prompt to the group was "Share a time you felt powerless." Aliyah spoke about her failed marriage. I thought, *Holy shit, she's been married before.* The prospects for us began looking slimmer. She was older and had been married; what experience could I offer?

I closed out the meeting.

"Great meeting facilitation," someone said, leaving.

I looked around to see if Aliyah had left and spotted her by the door. With great hesitation, I walked up to her to schedule a one-to-one meeting. *Something we do with all potential leaders*, I told myself to lower the emotional risk.

"*Assalaamu alaykum.*"

"*Walaykum assalaam*, hey," she smiled.

I felt the sweat on my torso bubbling underneath my skin and erupting to the surface.

"What'd you think?" I asked, sticking my hands in my pockets, not knowing what else to do with them.

"It was great, yeah. I wish more people would have been here, known about it, ya know?"

"Yeah, the turnout could have been better. Maybe you could help get the word out about the next one?"

"I'm about to start grad school so might not have much time to participate then, but I can help out now."

"Whatever you can contribute will help."

An awkward, unnerving silence settled between us. I lowered my gaze, and gave myself a silent pep talk. *No ulterior motives—just a one-to-one.*

"We should have a one-to-one, a chance to get to know one another and understand what issues we're passionate about," I explained breathlessly.

"Okay, when did you want to meet?" she asked.

That wasn't so bad.

"How about next Wednesday?"

"Sounds good. Should we exchange numbers in case something changes?"

She pulled out her phone and I recited my number. I stole a long glance as she typed. She had a small round head covered with a long pink scarf, soft cheeks and the pinkest lips I'd ever seen. She had a regal, dignified beauty I'd rarely seen. After punching in my number, she looked up. I shifted my gaze past her as if trying to find someone.

"Did you need to go talk to someone?" she asked pointing her thumb over her shoulder.

"No, just trying to see if brother Fareed is still here."

"Oh, okay. That's me calling so you can save my number in your phone."

"Sweet, thanks." It occurred to me that I could have gotten her number from the sign-in sheet. I smiled and wondered if she had realized it too. "Okay, gotta run. See you soon, *inshAllah.*"

"*Assalaamu alaykum!*" she waved timidly.

"*Walaykum assalaam,*" I said, strolling away as nonchalantly as I could.

She wanted to go somewhere beautiful near the water. I drove around San Francisco aimlessly until she looked up nearby beaches on her iPhone. "Here's one: China Beach. It's not far from here."

It had been a month since we'd met, but we spent so much time together that it felt that we'd always known each other. The parking lot was full, so we parked outside of a huge house with security cameras perched at each corner. The rusting, black wrought-iron fence was covered in spider webs.

"Wow. That's so strange," she said gazing up at the roof.

"What is?" I turned to look.

"Those cameras and this big gate," she replied.

"Why? They're just trying to protect themselves."

"It just looks paranoid. Like they don't want anyone here."

"Yeah, that's true. We're 'not welcome 'round these parts,'" I said, imitating a Southern accent.

We laughed and walked toward the beach, stopping to look at the Golden Gate Bridge. We hopped down the stairs like eager schoolchildren and climbed up a massive rock overlooking the water. We sat there for hours alternating between conversation about life dreams and a serene silence filled with the sounds of the ocean. We posed together for our smartphones, immortalizing an experience neither of us wanted to end.

"I feel beautiful," she said, beaming, her face turned toward the sun, reflecting its resplendence.

I wanted to kiss her. *I wonder when our first kiss will be.* I was too nervous to make a move. *When it happens, it will happen naturally.*

I opened her car door for her. She smiled her thanks. She was my lady.

Later, while telling me how much fun she'd had, she said, "I prayed for someone like you." I told her that I had prayed, too, while thinking to myself, *but I've been wrong before.*

When she said, "I need you," I felt a fluttering in my stomach I hadn't felt since Ashley. It was enchanting and terrifying.

After two months of courting, it felt like we were on the way toward marriage. In September—a few days after my twenty-fourth birthday—she brought up doing premarital counseling in December if "all continues to go well." *Women and their conditions,* I thought. She had made her intentions clear from the outset—she was looking for a spouse. I was ecstatic that I'd finally found a woman who knew what she wanted. I, too, was looking for a lifelong companion. We were both African American Muslims whose family histories included participation in the Nation of Islam. As a result, we had similar cultural and religious sensibilities. We had a passion for community. We just made sense. Everyone around us—at the *masjid*, on my job—agreed. Ms. Pierson—a widow in Bayview who loved to see young people in love—asked when we were getting married. When I told Imam Al-Amin that we were courting, he replied with a jovial grin, "I was hoping that would happen." My friend Ali supported us from the beginning, as did his wife, Martha.

One day in early October, a former colleague, Kisha, called me. She had accepted a job offer in Kenya but was homeless for the week prior to leaving. She'd been couch-surfing for weeks so I agreed to let her crash on my couch for a night. I forgot about it completely until the night of the stay. Aliyah and I were leaving an SFOP meeting at my office. She had become a volunteer leader in the organization after the initial meetings at the mosque, which gave us a halal excuse to spend more time together. We had yet to so much as embrace and hug; the sexual tension between us was palpable.

I parked in front of her place in Hayes Valley. She dreamed out loud, painting a picture of our life with emotional and hopeful words. I didn't feel the need to speak most of the time because she spoke for us both. This was the highest possible level of nonphysical intimacy. Our bodies ached to touch each other. She began stroking my hands and arms softly. I started to get hot and bothered. It was uncanny how cathartic the simplest touch could be, she said. I agreed, trying to conceal the bulge forming in my pants.

My phone buzzed. It was a text message from Kisha, "Hey, I'm on 22nd and Mission. Can you pick me up or do you want me to meet you somewhere else?" *Ah shit. I totally forgot about that!*

"Hey, sorry, I gotta go."

"Is everything okay?"

"I just forgot I have something to do."

"Oh . . . who was that?"

"My friend Kisha. I promised I'd let her stay on the couch for a night because she doesn't have a place to stay."

"Oh . . ." she said, taking her hand away, "I guess I'll see you later then."

"Hey, wait. What's the matter? You seem upset."

"You never told me about this," she said, tensing up, "I'm thinking, *Was he trying to hide this from me? Who is this girl?*"

"Whoa," I said, hands raised. "First, I wasn't trying to hide anything. If I was, I wouldn't have told you where I was going. Second, Kisha is a former colleague; she's my mom's age."

"Why does she have to stay at your house?"

"I thought it was the Muslim thing to do to provide shelter for her, so she doesn't have to sleep on the street!"

"Wow. I'm gonna go, but you need to talk to Imam Al-Amin about that," she said in an accusing tone.

"Talk to Imam Al-Amin about what?" I shot back.

"You just need to seek counsel on that, because I can't be the one to inform you."

"What are you saying? That I'm a bad Muslim for trying to help someone and I need to get guidance from the imam before Allah, in his wrath, smites me?"

"No," she let out an annoyed laugh, "just talk to the imam."

"All right, whatever."

She looked at me, mouth agape in surprise.

"Can you help me get my bike out of the backseat please?"

I got out of the car silently and walked her to the door. She thanked me and closed the door in my face. I was overwhelmed with guilt. *Was I wrong? How could I forget to tell her? Is it over just like that?* I told Kisha the story on the way home. She said that God had someone in store for me who wasn't insecure.

The next day, I asked Aliyah to meet me at Peet's Coffee. I ordered her a tea and a few madeleine cookies—her favorite. She sat with her hands over knees, looking aloof and prudish.

"I wanted to see how you're feeling about last night."

"Fine," she replied. "It's just a mental note that I've made."

"Are you thinking any different about us, because I still feel the same about you. Kisha is just a friend."

"My ex-husband knew a lot of women who were 'just friends.' Later, I found out he was taking them out." Her eyes shifted, never resting on me.

"I'm sorry that happened to you. But I'm not your ex-husband."

"I'm not saying you are. I'm sure you're telling the truth. All I'm saying is that you have relationships with a lot of different women and I don't—"

"What are you talking about?" I interrupted. "Most women I know are back home. I have hardly any friends here."

"I think we should take some time apart to work on ourselves. As I told you, I'm in graduate school and that's what I need to focus on."

"Okay, Aliyah."

"Is that it?"

"Yeah, that's it"

Aliyah was finished talking. What happened that night was something to be filed in her "mental notes" folder somewhere in that incomprehensible brain of hers. Graduate school was all she had time for and she felt it best that we "work on ourselves" (read: get your shit together, brotha). We had let our guards down because when we looked at each other we saw ourselves—wounded and afraid, longing and hopeful. Now, they were back up. The Kisha incident had set off all kinds of triggers in both of us. We began doubting whether the other could be trusted. We saw each other less, spending our time bickering, mostly about how I was too young to understand how life worked.

The end came late one night during an exasperating argument over God knows what.

"Would you listen for once? The key issue is that you aren't willing to meet me where I am."

"You're right. I'm not," she shot back.

"Wow . . . so I guess that's it," I said, stunned.

I got off of the phone and cried.

The New Year rolled around and here I was lonely and depressed. I returned to bong rips and pipe hits. Wake and bake, lunchtime liftoff, and evening equalizers became my daily routine. I had quit smoking weed after meeting Aliyah. She'd helped me see the upside of things, reminded me to turn to my Lord in times of crisis. I'd started praying again, studying Qur'an, and reflecting on the bounties of my Lord. Her leaving felt like a star's guiding light had burned out. It was also the two-year anniversary of my ex-girlfriend's betrayal, and I'd been abandoned in the dark again.

In February, I went to North Carolina to see family and found only chaos. My brother had started selling drugs. *I didn't come home for this shit*, I thought. A friend told me this could be a sign from God. I organized an intervention, prepping everyone, setting an agenda, a date, and a time. We sat in a circle in the living room where our high school graduation pictures adorned the wall. Everyone offered an emotional plea for my brother to stop. He agreed. The next night I went over to a friend's house and got high.

That trip was a watershed moment. During the intervention, my stepfather broke down and cried about his own past drug addictions in a plea for my brother to save himself. For the first time in my life, my stepfather was vulnerable to the point of tears. Seeing this moved me to tears, helped me understand him better, and, above all, emboldened me.

When I returned to California, I asked Aliyah to meet me in Golden Gate Park. I didn't really know what to say. I just knew I wanted to say *something* that would help her to understand me. As we walked together I felt tranquility descend onto me. Our conversation was light and jovial at first.

"Can I— Never mind," she began.

"What?"

"I'm embarrassed," she bowed her head.

"You don't have to say it if it makes you uncomfortable."

After a brief pause, she asked the question on her mind. "Are you seeing anyone right now?

I laughed, surprised. "No! Why?"

"If you were, it wouldn't be appropriate for us to be in touch like this."

"I'm not."

"Okay," she replied, repressing a smile.

Silence. But it wasn't the awkward silence that made me want to crawl out of my skin. It was a sacred silence in which the joy of each other's presence was enough. The sky became overcast and the wind picked up. We began making our way back to the car for refuge from the cold.

"I wanted to get a few things off my chest. I feel that our challenge has been that we do and say things, not realizing how it might trigger past experiences—"

"I feel like you do that a lot. I was going to bring it up earlier—" she interjected, defensively.

"What were you going to bring up?" I asked, curiosity piqued.

"You say things and I'm like, *Why would he say that?*"

"Can you be more specific?" I said, annoyance creeping into my voice.

"You tweeted something about your ex stripping—"

"What in the world are you talking about?" I pulled out my phone and started looking through my Twitter time line. "When was this?"

"I don't remember. But when I saw that, I unfollowed you because I said, *You know what, I don't need to get upset. I have the power to not look—*"

"Oh! Those were Drake lyrics. That wasn't about me. I'm not seeing anyone."

We arrived at the car and stood beside it arguing, the wind tossing her scarf across her face and making me shiver.

"Right, but did you ever stop and think, *How would this affect her if she read it?*" she shouted. Her eyes began tearing up, face reddening.

"You're blowing this out of proportion!" Something had tapped emotional triggers lodged deep down within both of us. My anxieties began resurfacing alongside her fears.

We got into the car, gazing out our own windows, not speaking. A million thoughts churned in my mind, distilling into one painful truth: a memory of self-destruction. I realized I had to let my guard down completely so she could finally see me and, perhaps, begin to understand.

"When Ashley left me I was in shambles. I couldn't sleep; I had no appetite for anything, including life. I stopped praying and started smoking weed to numb the pain." She turned around slowly and faced me, listening. I stared out the window, eyes glazing over.

"I started therapy, taking antidepressants, but that didn't help. The betrayal and loss felt like a poison I needed to drain. I felt like I would die if I didn't. The first time I used a kitchen knife, but it wasn't sharp enough to make more than a few scratches. The next time I used razor blades to cut up my wrists and my arms." My confession choked me up. I fought off the sobs and continued.

"I was so overwhelmed with grief that I was numb. Cutting became the only way I could feel anything. When I told my therapist. he asked, 'When did you begin to hate yourself so much?' I didn't know what to say. I never realized how much I didn't love myself."

I felt a calm wash over me. She sat in silence for a while, processing what she'd heard.

"You're not doing that anymore, are you?"

"No, I stopped a long time ago."

"Stephen, you are an amazing man. I've told you that before. But you have to believe that you are. That's what matters the most. No one else can truly love you, until you love yourself."

"I know," I said, turning to face her.

She was crying. Her eyes were red and her lip quivered. I knew that in that moment, she had heard me.

That day at the park reestablished our connection. It was as though I'd lowered the drawbridge, connecting our hearts. I finally let her in. Over the next several months we resumed our talks about marriage—except this time we weren't assessing compatibility. We were setting a date.

Our Way Lies Together

By Dan I. Oversaw

I married a Muslim. All thanks to Morgan Freeman.

I went to see *Robin Hood: Prince of Thieves* during its opening weekend at the Loews Natick theater in 1991 rather than waiting for it to play at the second-run Flick theater down at Sherwood Plaza. I mean, *Sherwood Plaza* for a Robin Hood movie, c'mon! (And, at half the price for a ticket.) But I was only fourteen, and had little time for poetic flourishes. I was too busy running to all the new experiences my New England suburban life offered to waste a moment on inessentials. The bad guy from *Die Hard* was fighting Kevin Costner—this was *important*.

Besides implanting that Bryan Adams song in my head for all the rest of my living days, *Robin Hood* turned out to have one lasting legacy: it introduced me to my first Muslim. Azeem Edin Bashir Al Bakir, wrongly convicted twelfth-century Muslim warrior played by Morgan Freeman, was a man of great wisdom, fearsome skills, and a rich baritone voice.

Okay, maybe, thinking about it, Azeem wasn't my first Muslim . . . considering that he is fictional, Freeman himself is agnostic, and the likelihood that I had encountered someone in my scant adolescent lifetime who practiced Islam. I grew up with Siddiquis, Patels, and Kasims in my classroom. They had to be . . . something, right? I just never took notice of them. Of basically anything outside my solipsistic field of vision. Given the early-nineties demographics of my hometown, the casual and offhand tolerance I enjoyed as a Reform Jew in a liberal community, there's every likelihood I knew a Muslim, a Buddhist, a Sikh. Azeem was, then, the first time I paid

attention to people outside of my narrow Jewish–Christian dichot-
omy. He was noble, principled, patient, deep, and lethal. (Trust me,
lethal means a lot to a red-blooded American boy.) In short, he was
cool. But, if he wasn't Jewish or Christian, then, outside of being a
Jedi, I had no category for him. And, anyway, I was too busy with
important things: X-Men comics, the Boston Celtics, unscrambling
the Spice channel signal on our cable box, and, closely related to
that, *girls*.

I had no way of knowing that Azeem/Morgan Freeman/Islam
would someday all be connected to a girl. A woman, actually, and
the mother of my child. Muna Ahmed Al-Yussif.

Nearly a decade later, when Muna mentioned that she was Muslim, *ding!* his image came into my head. ("Allah loves wondrous
variety," as Azeem said.) I had managed four years of college, a relo-
cation to Washington, DC, and entry into graduate school without
having to form any more sophisticated an understanding of Islam
than quotes from *Robin Hood*.

To be honest, though, it could have been worse; I had *Aladdin*,
True Lies, and VHS tapes of David Lynch's *Dune* all available to
skew my perceptions of Arab culture and Islamic principles. Not to
mention when camera crews flooded my campus in 1995 because
of its "Jewish identity," looking for student reactions after the assas-
sination of Israeli prime minister Yitzhak Rabin by a fellow Israeli
Jew. A number of friends seemed all too willing to give the reporters
heart-wrenching sound bites. I couldn't be bothered with politics or
the mumbo jumbo of religion. Jews, Israelis, Arabs, Muslims, they
were all caught up in the ugly swirl of religiosity, I felt. Besides, I
had important things to do. Like learn HTML. Or write a review for
the school newspaper. Truly important things were, by definition,
secular things.

By early 2001, though, "important" had, thank God, changed.
I was still apolitical, but I had a new appreciation of family and of
friends, now living several hundred miles away from them. Some

burgeoning desire to improve myself as a human being had sharply developed. I looked for opportunities to tap into a meaningful, larger discussion, not just be defined by my insulated, neurotic space. Who was benefitting from my holding an annual Oscar pool? What purpose did my massive comic book collection serve? I was attempting to move from the solipsist to the humanist, admittedly in very small steps. And yet, despite graduate study focusing on ancient lore, myth, and narrative, I still felt an allergy to religion. This was, I know now, a limitation: my aversion to religion kept me in a little life of easy things and overblown cares. In the ten years since I had seen *Robin Hood*, little had changed when it came to personal spiritual expansion.

One day, though, changed me a great deal. It was January 2001, and, to offset the cost of my grad degree in English literature, I was working in the school's administrative offices. Not a bad job and one that had suited me fine all fall semester. It was on this morning that I was introduced to my new workmate, Muna.

"Where I come from, Christian, there are women of such beauty, that they can possess a man's mind so that he would be willing to die for them," marveled Azeem.

It wasn't love at first sight—but it was fascination. She had an easy smile, a kind laugh, and these amazing, *impossible* eyes. I think I'm supposed to describe them as "almond-shaped," but I hate almonds and I love these eyes. Brown and rich, with a glint of enchantment. I can admit now, a dozen years later, that I may have caught a glimpse of Princess Jasmine in them, a twinge of exotic, Orientalist allure. Yet, I very easily overcame my programming, hacked my Disney-fication, as I grew to know the woman behind them.

The courtship was a literal one: I invited her to play racquetball. Innocent enough, right? Here's a doughy, lapsed Jew from Boston inviting his lovely, curvy coworker out to a platonic match at the campus gym. There's no romance, no ulterior motive, and certainly no head game. I was safe and eager to make a friend. Muna, to my astonishment, agreed. Years later, at our wedding, the maid of honor would gently jibe that, for the first few months of what would become my "wooing" of Muna, the two of them referred to me by the title "Racquetball Boy."

"A wise man once said: 'There are no perfect men in the world; only perfect intentions.'"

I didn't intend to fall in love with Muna. She was beautiful and enthralling, no doubt, but racquetball was never Stage One of some romance strategy. (Honestly, has *anyone* ever used racquetball as some opening move in a romantic gambit?) And it wasn't our court time that did it, not directly. Two things, one large and one small, drew me to her.

First, she challenged me. I played a mediocre game of racquetball, and she quickly caught up to that—but that's not what I mean. Our games sometimes went late, and we soon started to grab the occasional bite to eat afterward. (You know, to offset any calories we had actually lost.) It was at The Tombs, the landmark restaurant on the fringe of Georgetown's campus, where we sat, ate, and talked. I told her my stories, which were relatively easy ones to tell: suburban Boston kid, liberal arts major, pop-culture junkie. Her life had been far, far more compelling: American mother and Arab father, born and raised in the Gulf region, lost father suddenly to heart condition, saw rockets fly overhead during Desert Storm, relocated to rural U.S., reinvented herself in college, and was putting herself through grad school.

She was bilingual, well traveled, and sharp. Muna had views on international affairs but also a cringing dirty joke to unleash upon the unsuspecting (namely, "What do two tampons say as they walk down the street? [PUNCH LINE REDACTED]"). Sibling rivalry with an older brother had brought out her inner tomboy, her video game nerd, and even a Dungeons & Dragons streak; college-age rebellion had cultivated a rave-dancing, drum-and-bass-grooving modern woman. Any stereotypes or exotic fantasies I may have had of her were quickly blown away. Here was a woman like none I had encountered before. She was, in a word, formidable.

"Where I come from, we talk to our women."

The second thing that drew me to her was that, as much as she would attempt to stay composed and only "glisten" when we played racquetball, her sweat smelled like faint, sweet pumpkin. Pumpkin! It was so charming and so unusual that I tried to hold on to that scent in my olfactory memory hours after we had each gone home.

Until Muna, I had been in retreat. I had been thinking of leaving grad school, of going home to Boston. Life outside of my college cocoon had rubbed me raw. It was all the usual stuff, I suppose: working for an income, living on my own, and having no social safety net. What made it especially hard for me was the well-hidden, very shameful anxiety disorder that I had been combatting since adolescence—a crippling panic that would sometimes grab me, the frenzied loss of control that plagued me. Over the years, I immersed myself in film, books, television, and popular culture as a method of casually combating it, but it was too big and too daunting to maintain so far from home. It left me safe nowhere and comfortable with no one. With such a primal fear always ready to erupt, it was difficult to feel fully human.

I explained my anxiety disorder and sadness to Muna using film metaphors. I likened myself to Jack Nicholson in *As Good as It Gets*, as a man whose mind got in the way of his search for happiness. I returned to Morgan Freeman, this time as Red in *The Shawshank Redemption*, paralleling how the various strategies I'd crafted to avoid panic attacks left me as trapped as his "institutionalized man." I never thought I would be free of it and, if I ever was, I didn't know who I would be. I chose not to hope—because, as Red warned, "Hope is a dangerous thing. Hope can drive a man insane."

Muna was calm, compassionate, and direct. I couldn't retreat, she told me; I had to keep pushing. Her friendship and, later, her affection, became inspiring. Her faith, too, encouraged me. Her beliefs were a personal experience for her. Rather than being defined by mosques, alcohol, or pork, Muna demonstrated the power and effervescence of Islam. God may not be within us, but the divine can connect intimately with that which is within us. She never proselytized, never foregrounded her religion in any of our interactions; it was her example and depth of thought that compelled me to reach for more.

Too afraid to get in a car, I would ride my bicycle all the way to her apartment on cold nights. I would confide in her things it had taken years to tell friends. From this, I felt stronger. As Jack's character said in *As Good as It Gets*, she made me "want to be a better man." And like *Shawshank* reminded viewers, in addition to being a dangerous thing, hope can also set one free.

"Get busy living or get busy dying," Red decides. "That's god-damn right."

If I were to liken myself to any movie object it would have to be Andy Dufresne's rock hammer in *Shawshank*. Day by day, I scratched my way into Muna's life. Andy used the tiny rock-sculpting pick to carve himself free of the penal institution. My quiet perseverance made a slow path to Muna's core. It wasn't that I was subtle; she knew I was there, was interested, and was smitten. But I was also the harmless "Racquetball Boy" with mind demons of his own. Who knew that being steadfast and unabashedly reliable could have a charm all its own? And, *un*like the leftover nub of the rock hammer by the time Andy escaped, the slow dig to my new life made me stronger, not weaker.

By August 2005, my life had transformed from one of self-imposed limits to one of possibility. I had stayed in Washington, DC, to complete graduate school, to work at the college, and to immerse myself in the study of religious narrative. The agnostic disdain I had felt was washing away, and I was already thinking about a PhD that would somehow incorporate religious study. Muna and I had begun dating, then moved in together. When people asked how it was for a Muslim and Jew to live together as a couple, I'd joke that it was like that line from *Ghostbusters:* "Dogs and cats! Living together! Mass hysteria!" In truth, we took a lot of comfort and strength from each other, especially in the wake of the September 11 attacks and ensuing jingoistic Islamophobia. Rather than retreating, we actively chose to return to Boston together that year.

(We also got cats. Named them Bamf and Snikt, sound effects from the X-Men comics. Her idea, I swear! Do you see why I love this woman?)

I won't paint our relationship as a fairy tale: like Morgan says in *Se7en,* "Hell, love costs. It takes effort and work." But it had become the core of the *important stuff* that now shaped my life. In August of the year we moved to Boston, as we were sitting on Nantasket Beach, I nervously asked Muna to marry me. Even though it was too dark for her to see the ring, she said yes without reservation.

Our wedding was a blend of traditions, a civil ceremony officiated by my best friend (the son of a rabbi), featuring both Jewish and Islamic elements. When our daughter was born a few years later, the little girl took my surname but was given an Arabic name: Ayah, a sign from God. And she was—she *is.*

In fact, I now see every aspect of my life, from the major moments to the most cheesy movie quote, as some sign from God. Yet, all those signs, in all their forms, require effort and dedication. Take it from Morgan as God, in *Bruce Almighty:* "People want me to do everything for them. What they don't realize is *they* have the power. You want to see a miracle, son? Be the miracle."

Muna admits now that she suspected the same thing I did—that starting in 2005, I was on a path to become Muslim myself. It had taken years to move from being a scared jokester to a responsible man, a process that included therapy for my anxiety disorder, reprioritizing, and flat-out work. Moving toward Islam would take a similar journey on my terms—my Islam. I kept my birth name, I pray frequently but not daily, and I still hold an abiding respect for Judaism. These rituals, to me, never defined whether one was Muslim or not. My practice and my household only determine what kind of Muslim I am—how I fulfill the promise and the gifts God has given me. But, most especially, the love I'm fortunate enough to enjoy.

As Azeem, Morgan Freeman may have exposed me to Muslims and to the idea of religious pluralism. But I didn't know Islam until I met Muna. Whatever God's plan may be for us, separate or together, I now welcome it instead of fear it.

I married a Muslim, and, now, I am a Muslim. Thanks *in part* to Morgan Freeman.

Echoes

By Mohammed Samir Shamma

I read the words "Vista Point" on the highway sign and exited. It wasn't my destination, merely a viewing stop along the way. Since turning forty, I've discovered that life's little moments can be quite breathtaking. I paused in front of the panorama and considered the sequence of events that had brought me here—graphing the phases of my life, from childhood to marriage and fatherhood, against the expansion and contraction of my heart. I have renewed gratitude for this muscle—for the blood it draws into itself and ejects, for the deep, low recitation of my heartstrings. After replaying my memories over and over again, the result is the same. There is an indelible harmony between my Muslim identity and my heart—a song filled with notes of sin, pain, devotion, love, and salvation—the five pillars of my personal cardiac cycle.

Sin

The first phase of a heartbeat is known as early diastole. It is when the semilunar valves close and the atrioventricular valves open, and the whole heart is relaxed.

I was five when I first learned I was Muslim. It was after I'd spent a relaxing preschool day as the proud master of my domain, the sandlot. I created paved roads with small plastic shovels, molded houses without interiors, constructed schools and churches without students or followers. As I toiled away at my miniature representation of the world, my shovel exposed a shiny object in the sand. It was a gold cross pendant on a necklace. Immediately, I cleaned it off and placed it around my neck. The crucifix swung below my heart.

Moments later, I saw my father's olive green Plymouth Valiant pull up in the school driveway. I ran to greet him.

"Daddy! Daddy! Look what I found today."

He knelt down and caught me in his arms. "What is it? Show me, *habibi*," he said in an English accent, the result of British schooling in Egypt.

"Look. It's a necklace just like all the other kids wear," I said with wide innocent eyes.

"Oh, wow! That's a big necklace. May I see it?"

I took it off and handed it to him. He suddenly turned and gave it to my preschool teacher.

"Hey, that's mine," I yelled as she took it and walked away.

"*Habibi*. It's not yours. Someone lost it and she will help them find it. Now *yalla*."

I followed him to the car and got into the front passenger seat. He drove off, pulled into the left turn lane, and stopped at a red light.

"Do you know what we are?" He said looking down at me.

"What?" I asked as I scratched my chest, as if feeling for the cross.

"We are Muslims. We are not Christians." He seemed to be struggling for the right words to say—words that a five-year-old might understand.

I listened, but gave him no response.

"Only Christians wear that necklace." Pointing his finger at me, he said, "You are not Christian. You are Muslim. Your name is Mohammed." He shook his finger at me. "You cannot wear this."

I accepted my faith, but cried silently. I loved that necklace. I adored the feeling of shiny gold on my skin. I felt guilty inside, as if I'd misbehaved at birth. I didn't want to be different.

The next day, my mother picked me up from school. I ran to her as I always did after a long day of play.

"Mommy! Mommy! Mommy!"

"Oh my Heavens! Look at how dirty you are," she said in that native Texan accent of hers. "Come on now. Let's go home and clean you up."

I hopped into the passenger seat and waited for her to sit at the wheel.

"Mommy?"

"Yes, Maddy?" Her pet name for me. "What is it?"

"Are you a Christian or a Muslim?"

"I'm a . . . Christian," she said with slight hesitation.

"Do you have to pray?"

"Of course I pray. I pray in church on Sundays."

"You don't pray all day like Muslims?"

She laughed. "Well, no. But I pray in my heart all the time."

"Mommy?" I said, watching another church pass by the car window.

"Why can't I be a Christian?"

Pain

The second phase of the heartbeat is atrial systole. The
atrium contracts, causing the blood to flow into the ventricle.

My father had a change of heart after bearing witness to that cross around my neck. He made it his mission to teach me and every other Muslim child in the city their *deen*. He networked all over Houston and invited other families to our house for Friday night Islamic school. Each week cars arrived on our street like blood cells coming into the heart from the remote capillaries of city streets. Our front door became a one-way valve, opening and closing to the parade of proud parents flowing in with hot food to eat and children to teach. My mother, now a Muslim herself, greeted the guests with the customary, "*Assalamu Alaykum!* Welcome! Come on in," and showed them into our tiny ventricular living room. Folding chairs occupied the space where our coffee table and couch sat; whiteboards hung from the wall behind the television, and stacks of the Qur'an covered the adjacent dining room table.

One Friday night, when I was in the second grade and in class with other seven-, eight-, and nine-year-olds, I grew bored of all the Islamic activity around me. I leaned my chair back, listening secretly through the thin membrane of the partition. The fourth and final chamber, immediately behind me, was reserved for the most advanced students.

"Who can tell me what verse sixteen of *Sura al-Qaf* says?" The voice of the instructor was always loud and clear. It was followed by silence. "No one? How about you, Qaseem?"

I could hear the sound of pages rustling. Then a voice echoed out of the silence: "And We have already created man and know what his soul whispers to him, and We are closer to him than his jugular vein."

"Pay attention." My father's hand came from nowhere and gently but firmly set my chair back down, sitting me upright in my seat.

"Daddy." My wisp of an index finger beckoned his ear.

"What?" he asked, eyes locked into mine. He could tell that I wanted him closer to me, so he conceded. "What is it?"

"Daddy, after everyone leaves, can we watch movies?" I was pointing to the Bell & Howell silent-film projector and screen sitting on the floor next to me.

"Maybe. We'll see. Did you finish your letters? Show me how to write your name."

"Okay," I said as I leaned over the card table and carved out the *meem, hah, meem,* and *dal* of Mohammed for him.

"*Shaatir.*"

"So can we?"

"Can we what?"

"Watch movies on the projector?"

"We'll see. We'll see. *InshAllah.*"

I knew he would forget. He wasn't concerned with the past or the present. His heart bore the weight of the future. He was managing the transition of the school to a new location: a one-story office building that could be converted into a prayer hall, a small school with administrative offices, a shelter, a kitchen, and a parking lot. But this was the lighter of the two loads. He was also managing another transition, a drastic career change that involved relocating our family to Egypt.

My father died in October 1981, before the move. They found him on the floor of his office just hours after he gave his two-week notice. His heart had failed him. He was forty-six. I was nine.

My mother sat my brother and me on the bed and looked at us through her damp, Southern Gothic eyes.

"Boys, your daddy died today. He had a heart attack at work." She couldn't finish the sentence. She sounded like a car screeching to a halt trying to avoid a wall of tears.

The look I gave her must have been shocking. I can only say this now, as a parent of two children myself. The eyes of children are windows into their hearts. They're more telling than their actions or lips. My mother's face turned pale and she put both hands over her mouth, muffling her shrill cry. I ran over and hugged her. I hated to see her cry. I wanted to cry too, but my anger burned away the tears. Dejected and contracted, the nine-year-old boy in me vowed never to let her cry again.

Devotion

The third phase involves isovolumic ventricular contraction. The ventricles begin to contract, the atrioventricular valves close, and the semilunar valves are not yet open. There is no change in volume.

My mother took us to Egypt for a visit in the summer of 1982. She wanted us to meet our paternal family—voices we had heard over the phone at odd hours of the night, strangers yelling their love for us over the static, relatives we'd never seen. Initially, it felt like we'd entered another reality.

"Look! There they are. They're waving to you." My mother was excited to see my father's family again after sixteen years.

As we emerged into the arrivals hall, the strangers rushed us and began hugging and kissing me.

"*Alhamdila ala salaama! Wahashtoonah*," they repeated, "Welcome! Welcome! We missed you so much!" between suffocating kisses and hugs.

They stuffed us off into an old European taxi and brought us to a rundown apartment building in Shoubra, an aging suburb of Cairo that flourished in the 1940s and '50s. We walked three flights of stairs and stopped at a weatherworn door. My cousin Ashraf opened it and we filed past him into an apartment that was a time capsule from the '60s.

"What is this place?" I asked.

"It's where your father and I used to live," she said proudly.

"You left Texas to live here?"

"That's right. We lived here for two years, before moving to Houston."

"Where's the refrigerator?" I asked.

"We don't have one yet," my mother said.

"But I want a Coke," I whined.

"Sorry, but we're having tea right now."

"What about something to eat? Do they have Doritos?"

"No. But they have pita bread and cheese."

"No, thank you."

"Can I watch TV? Maybe *The Facts of Life* is on? Or *Diff'rent Strokes*? What channel is NBC?"

"There's no TV here. We can see about getting one later."

"Mom! What am I gonna do here?"

My annoying questions continued into the morning and through my first days in Egypt. I wouldn't see my home again for another two months.

My mother was in heaven on earth. In 1964 she'd abandoned her secretary's desk at the IRS office in Lubbock, Texas, and bought a one-way ticket to Egypt to marry my father, her pen pal of twelve years. I could see the remnants of their honeymoon in her eyes as she encouraged me to come out of my shell and speak with my cousins. We spent our first few days as tourists, which eased the transition. We rode camels and horses at the Pyramids, shopped at Khan el-Khalili, and wandered aimlessly through the Egyptian Museum.

"Why can't we see the mummies?" I asked my mother as we passed the closed entrance to the royal mummy room.

"I don't know. Ashraf is asking the guard right now."

I watched Ashraf as he spoke to the uniformed guard. Their hands spoke louder than their mouths.

Then suddenly, I couldn't hear anything. My ears were ringing and I felt dizzy. As I tried to shake it off, I flashed back to the night of my father's funeral. I stood before the empty pit as they lowered his coffin into the ground. One of the straps came loose and the door of the coffin flew open in front of me. In the split second before the door closed, I recognized the shape of my father's head underneath the white burial cloth.

"Maddy?" My mother grabbed me by the shoulders and turned me around. "What's gotten into you?"

"What, me?" I said as I pulled myself to the surface. My mother's concern helped calm my nerves and I eased under the umbrella of her devotion.

"The mummies have been put in the basement. They're locked up and can't be seen right now."

"I don't want to see the mummies anymore. Let's go."

I decided not to ask any more questions. I was afraid of having another flashback. I had to control myself and think of something other than death and my have-nots. My heart gave in and grew slightly more Freudian that day, and every day thereafter. I forced myself to speak Arabic with my cousins to overcome our language barrier. My mother's eyes began to light up. As I prayed and recited Qur'an with them, her smile widened even more. The month of Ramadan arrived and I chose to fast for the first time that summer. The suffering was sweet as long as there was a reward; her smile was the best dish on the table for *iftar*.

When we returned to Texas, I felt proud standing up in front of my fifth-grade class and telling them about my summer in Egypt and my extended family overseas. That night I took the place of my father, reciting *al-Fatiha* and leading the evening prayer.

Love

The fourth phase is known as ventricular ejection. The ventricles are empty and contracting, and the semilunar valves are open.

In the years following my father's death I slowly realized that my devotion to family and religion, like my own blood supply, was limited. After *isha* was over and my mother and brother were asleep, I would stare into my father's bathroom mirror at the signs of puberty arriving on my skin, and hear them in my voice, praying for manhood to come soon. By the eighth grade, I thought I was ready. I prayed to Allah that a girl like Stephanie, Sarah, or Angela would notice me and that my mother wouldn't learn about the semi-innocent games of truth or dare, or the middle school parties with make-out sessions to the sounds of mix tapes.

During my freshman year of high school I was lucky enough to have friends with cars—Muslim friends who kept my mother blind to the binge drinking and sleepovers. She eventually caught on and tried to hide her pain. Her angelic son was dead and all that was left was a hormonal halfling heaving under the covers with heathen girls. She tried to rein me back with a fire-and-brimstone version of Islam that she, the former Baptist from pure-white West Texas cotton country, could relate to. I tried to placate her, but I would never be as good as my father. I was a native Texan with an Arab name—the son of a dead Muslim survived by his proselyte.

I was seventeen when I packed all my necessities along with my insecure Arab Muslim baggage and headed off to the University of Texas at Austin with my girlfriend. We'd been attached at the hip since we first met in our sophomore year of high school. But our rocky relationship began to fail during our first year of college, when she was struggling with the freshman fifteen, and with the fifteen she got on her chemistry test. She could no longer pass her classes and was facing expulsion. It ended in a typical out-of-control shouting match.

"Look, I don't want to do this anymore. I'm sick and tired of fighting with you." My throat burned from all the screaming.

"Well, what are you going to do about it? Break up with me?"

"Yes," I said calmly after a long pause. I left her apartment and never went back. My heart was racing over the plunge I had just taken—the "yes" that I'd never uttered before. My replies were usually, "No. That's not what I mean. I'm just worried about you." The truth was that I was also failing. I was failing at living in sin. I would also fail engineering, business, and premed. I too was on scholastic probation and faced expulsion if I didn't repair my GPA.

My only option was to go after the low-hanging fruit. I registered for Arabic 1.0 in the fall of my junior year, and after the first two weeks of class, I had learned more than in all the Friday nights and Sunday mornings in Islamic school. The "A" in Arabic boosted my GPA and gave me the right to call myself Mohammed. That spring I racked up another set of excellent grades in Arabic, geography, anthropology, and the history of the Middle East. There was something about those Middle Eastern studies classes. We just clicked.

"Mohammed, this is a great paper on the negative impact of the Aswan High Dam," said my geography professor, who had nearly lost his life in a desert flash flood.

"Mohammed, I love your analysis of liminality and the ritual of Muslim prayer," said my anthropology professor, whose husband was Moroccan.

"Mohammed, is Shamma your family name? Are you Jewish?" asked my adviser from Tel Aviv.

The interest in me, whether genuine or not, didn't stop with the faculty.

"Mohammed, you should sign up for Model Arab League," said Blanca, whose boyfriend was Lebanese.

"Mohammed, will you play the tabla for us?" said Debbie the part-time student, part-time belly dancer, who assumed I must've played throughout my life.

This royal treatment boosted my ego. Over the next few years, I gained a newfound confidence that I'd lost somewhere between my father's death and denying my faith and mother's wishes. I was proudly rediscovering the buried Muslim tomb of my American Egyptian identity. I wanted to meet others like myself.

"You're Heidi. Right?" She nodded and gave me a cautious smile as I singled her out of the crowd of students leaving the classroom.

"I'm Mohammed. I sit behind you."

"What's up?" She said in a casual manner.

All of a sudden, I wasn't prepared. Five years of studying and learning and now I didn't have anything to say. The words were locked up inside me. I fumbled for a key, but couldn't find one. Instead I tried to pick the lock with the closest object I could find.

"That's a really cool necklace. Where did you get it?"

"Thanks," she said softly. She made a motion to cover it, but then her hand backed away. "It's the goddess Isis. My mom got it for me—in Egypt." Her pharaonic charm had been working on me even before she opened her lips. I didn't know what ancient Egyptian god she had dangling from her neck, but the shy, downward gazing statue on her neck guided me, like a pair of wings.

Her hands were right to be cautious. I was trying to read her and translate my feelings into meaning. "That's cool," I said. I wanted to know where she came from, but was trying not to trip over myself and blurt out the question. "What did your mom like best about it?"

"She knew I liked ancient Egypt."

"But what did she like about Egypt? Did she go for the pyramids? Or the mosques?"

"What are you talking about? She wasn't a tourist. We're from Egypt."

You idiot, I said to myself. Here I am, outside of a class on Middle East history and I'm acting like I don't know where the brownskinned, curly headed girl with the Isis necklace is from. I had to play it off.

"No way! That's so cool. Where are you from in Egypt?"

"Cairo," she said blankly.

"Yeah, but where in Cairo?"

"You know Cairo?"

"I know enough to get lost." Wait a minute. That sounded better in my head than on my lips.

"It's technically outside of Cairo. You wouldn't know it."

Whew! I thought. I must be doing something right. She's still talking.

"Try me," I said.

"Maryuitiyya." The name of the canal street rolled off her tongue in perfect Egyptian Arabic. She was legit.

"Maryuitiyya?" I said as I struggled with the Arabic pronunciation. "That's where I was this summer. My uncle lives on that street."

"You lived on Maryuitiyya Street?"

"It's true. He lives next to the mosque on the west side of the road, next to the KFC parking lot, about five hundred feet from Faisal Street."

"Impressive."

I gave her my phone number and said we should hang out for coffee sometime.

"Sounds great," she said as she knelt down to get something out of her backpack. To my surprise, she tore the corner of a page off her notebook, wrote her number down, and gave it to me.

Salvation

During the fifth stage, "isovolumic ventricular relaxation," pressure decreases, no blood enters the ventricles, the ventricles stop contracting and begin to relax, and the semilunar valves close due to the pressure of blood in the aorta.

I sat in front of the blue fountain at the main entrance of Stanford Medical Center, distilling everything that had just happened. I was dreading the call to my wife. I thought about breaking the news when I got home, but one look at my face and Heidi would know everything. What would she say? What could she say? We'd known each other for eighteen years now: married for the past fifteen, parents for the past five. I was building up the nerve to call her, just like the time I'd rehearsed the lines in my head to pump myself up to call her from a payphone in the basement of the UT campus tower.

"Hey, Heidi. Man, I'm so wired on all that coffee and studying. I had to call you to relax." *No, too cheesy.*

How about, "I'm getting a study group together. You're welcome to join." *She'd know it was a lie.*

My bride, with whom I exchanged rings at the footsteps of the pyramids, honeymooned in Italy, and returned to Europe, year after year, walking its cobblestone streets and admiring its beauty, would be scared to death of losing her husband and the father of her children.

"Hi. It's me." Just me, I thought, the real me—without rehearsal.

"Hi, Mohammed. What did the doctor say? Did he order the DNA test?" I could hear our children playing in the background. She was anxious to hear good news, news that everything was fine, that Kareem and Leila would be fine as they waited for me to return.

"I have it. He showed me the MRI and I saw it."

The *it* was the pear-shaped scar tissue in the middle of my heart. It was echoing the involuntary beat signal as it passed through the muscle. It was the cause of my father's death. Like the religion he had tried to instill into my identity, this was his gift to me.

"Are you sure? Isn't the DNA test more accurate?" She was good at scrutinizing. It's one of her traits that I love. It's also how she survived the PhD program in Egyptian art and archaeology at Cal.

"He said he didn't need to see a test. It was right there on the screen."

"But what about the other cardiologists?"

"He said they misdiagnosed me. They only see patients with hypertrophic cardiomyopathy once or twice a year. Dr. Knowles said he sees three to five patients each week."

"So does this mean you need a defibrillator, like your brother?"

"Yes."

"When is the surgery?"

"I have to meet with the surgeon first. And the genetics counselor also wants to meet us."

"So, how do you feel about everything?"

"I'm scared, but only about having the surgery. I'm optimistic about the defibrillator."

"Why?"

"Because Dr. Knowles said it will listen to my heart and save me in the event of a heart attack. It will give me a 98 percent chance at a normal life."

"What is a normal life?"

"A life where I get to die at a ripe old age, like everybody else."
I could tell she wasn't convinced—no *alhamdulillah*. I wasn't convinced yet either. I didn't really know what a normal life was, but I didn't want to show it.

I've had my implantable cardioverter-defibrillator for almost six months now. When necessary, my cardiologist can read my every heartbeat from the moment he fired it up inside me—my "rebirth." He tells me not to obsess about it, but I hear the echoes of my life like the very graphs printed before the doctor. I sing atop the peaks, roar in the valleys, and weep in the caves I've created along the way. Family dance time on Friday nights or Sunday mornings helps me forget about my midlife crisis. As my five-year-old son, Kareem, mimics Heidi's crazy hipline moves, I spin my daughter, Leila, round and around until we collapse together, dizzy with laughter. Then the world stops spinning, and I catch my breath.

Becoming Family

By Randy Nasson

If you don't try to fly,
And so break yourself apart,
You will be broken open by death,
When it's too late for all you could become.

—Jalāl ad-Dīn Muhammad Rūmī

Sitting in uncomfortable silence on our fire escape, she turned to look at me as I exhaled. The smoke clouded the air between us. I was not going to speak first. I almost never do, especially when I am in the wrong.

"Do you love me, Randy?"

This wasn't the "I'm just asking because I want to hear you say it" variety that warrants an affectionate "Of course I do," followed with a hug and a kiss. No, this time, she really wanted to know. She needed to know because she didn't know.

"Yes."

"Are you sure?"

That stung, but I could hardly blame her. "Yes."

"Do you still want to be in this marriage?" she asked. "If you don't, then be honest and we can have that discussion."

It would've been easier to run. I don't deny that I was tempted. I was caught in a lie and my guilt was festering into cowardice. I could take the out she offered me, move back to Boston, and resume my life minus the accountability of being a husband. That would have been the easy choice. Yet, I knew it was the wrong one.

"I do want to be in this marriage. I want to make this work."

Sitting fearful and fragile, I retreated to one of my favorite memories from our courtship the previous year. It was October 2001, a month after we'd met. Ayesha was visiting friends in San Francisco and asked if I wanted to join her for the city's annual Halloween party. I held her in my arms as the revelers in the Castro dissolved into a blur of color and muffled voices, a pulsing kaleidoscope with her eyes fixed at the center. Those eyes that said "I love you" even though her lips had yet to; that gazed longingly into mine on the beach in Mendocino later that weekend; that said "yes" to my spontaneous marriage proposal two months later.

Those were heady days. I was completely in love, unguarded and fearless.

That was fifteen months ago, before we married and moved from Boston to San Francisco in search of a new life together. Before the lack of community exposed how fragile a new relationship can be. Before I let her down.

The distinct advantage to getting married young, or to not having premarital relationships: you carry no baggage to pollute your marriage. You have a clean slate. I did not. I lied about something I should have been honest about. When Ayesha found out, she was furious and devastated. I didn't know if I could regain her trust, but I loved her too much not to try.

I knew that I wanted to make things right. What I didn't know was that the journey to reconciliation would require radical transformation. Flowers, romantic getaways, and nights out dancing—none of these was going to work.

To redefine us, I had to start by redefining myself.

A few weeks later, Ayesha once again turned to look at me, this time across the admitting room at Saint Francis Hospital, where she sat in a wheelchair, inexplicably unable to walk or stand. Her eyes said, "I'm scared and alone because I have nobody here but you and I don't know if I can trust you." As they wheeled her away to an examination room, I was sent to fetch her personal items: a toothbrush, pajamas, a change of clothes.

When I awoke that morning, I'd turned over and seen her trying to hold herself up against the wall, struggling to make her way across the room. When it was clear that this wasn't merely a case of her leg or foot being asleep, we quickly made our way to a nearby doctor's office. After an expedited examination, the doctor arranged for an emergency admission.

He suspected Guillain-Barré syndrome, a rare, mysterious paralysis. We had to get her to the ICU to start treatment before things got worse.

After gathering Ayesha's belongings at our apartment, I sat stunned, holding the phone to my ear. When my mother said, "Hello" in her usual happy and inviting voice, I couldn't speak.

"Hello?" she repeated.

"Hi, Mom."

Those were the only words I could muster before I began sobbing uncontrollably. I don't know why I made the call from the bathroom; perhaps it felt safer, cleaner, with nearby water, towels, and Band-Aids. I tried to pull myself together while Mom called my name tenderly.

"Randy? Honey what's wrong? Are you okay?"

I just wanted to fall to the floor. I wanted my mother there to hold me and tell me everything was going to be all right.

"It's Ayesha," I said. "She's in the hospital. . . . She can't walk. . . . I don't know what's happening."

"In sickness and in health . . ." I had heard that phrase so many times; the "old-age clause" in the marriage vow.

Not that I recall any specific vows—other than my affirmation that I agreed to be her husband. It was all such a blur. I was utterly bewildered, having landed in Pakistan the day before, attended our *mehndi* that night, and then come to her family's house for the official marriage ceremony the next morning.

Remembering our wedding the year before, I sat there feeling helpless in her hospital room. I didn't know how to support her in her time of need.

The door opened and her father walked in with a warm and soothing smile. For the first time in days, she expressed sincere relief because someone had finally arrived on whom she could rely.

I was her husband, but I wasn't family.

Family is not created through blood ties or marital contracts. Family is an exchange of intimacy, trust, sympathy, counsel, and caregiving that connects our souls.

For years I kept my own family at arm's length in pursuit of a fierce independence from intrusion, concern, guilt, or anything that would complicate my pursuit of self-indulgence. I was always looking for a good opportunity or a good time, and if you didn't want to come along with me that was fine as long as you didn't stand in my way.

That's not to say that I never forged any meaningful relationships. But looking back, I recognize that when the people closest to me were in need, I wasn't able to fully listen or be present because I was self-consumed, worried about how I was being impacted or busily formulating a response instead of focusing on the other person.

Over the next few weeks, Ayesha recovered, though we never received a firm diagnosis. A victory, but still shallow and incomplete, like my resolution to be a better husband.

Later that summer, we moved to a more spacious apartment that was closer to her office. But a new address can't help you escape your problems when your problems are within yourself, and forgetting the past—which isn't really possible—does not heal a wounded heart.

By the time my father came to visit, later that fall, I was deeply depressed. A few rounds of marital counseling had helped us diffuse the fighting and afforded civil discourse, but our communication remained sparse. I wallowed in private misery, wondering if my future would consist of unending dutiful days. Despite my sincere repentance, things weren't better. Trust takes years to rebuild.

One evening during his stay, Dad and I went out together. I had never talked with him about what was going on between Ayesha and me. But I laid it all out on the table: the transgression, stress, counseling, the near-divorce. I needed advice badly. What I got instead was a stunning reflection.

He responded with some accounts of his own marital issues, complained for a bit about his wife, and talked in abstract clichés about the challenges of dealing with women and marriage. Instead of engaging me about my situation, he vented about his problems. I was briefly infuriated, ready to lash out, when it hit me.

"This is what she experiences when we talk," I realized. When she reached out to me, I remained too consumed with my own sadness and confusion to listen, to be present, or to offer comfort.

My insight was painful. Not only had I been deaf for the duration of our relationship, but it became clear that I had been so throughout my adult life.

I shared my epiphany with Ayesha, but it took several months of faithful attentiveness before her skepticism began to give way.

Mendocino had always been a favorite romantic getaway of ours: the salt-worn clapboard siding on the mid-nineteenth-century homes that were now bed-and-breakfasts, the rhythmic lapping of the ocean against the shoreline, the quaint shops and the cozy rooms with private fireplaces and hot tubs. Soon after my realization and subsequent resolve to be a better listener, we spent the entire weekend in a secluded cabin, happy to be alone together, talking about our future and wishing we could live in Mendocino forever.

When she spoke, she had my full attention. It wasn't easy at first, but I continued to make the effort of tuning into her words and feelings. I was ready to be a better husband, and for the first time, I was ready to listen, sympathize, and act on her behalf.

A few months later, lying in bed one morning, Ayesha turned
to me.

"Randy?"

"Yes, babe?" She looked lovely as the early light fell on her face.
But the look in her eyes told me something was wrong.

"I can't feel my feet."

Repairing our marriage was one thing. Our real trial was about
to begin.

I sat on the floor of our bedroom exhausted, saddened, and enraged.
Behind me she lay on her side moaning in pain. She had been in
great pain all evening, her spinal cord inflamed in the area near
where she had had previous exacerbations. This was shaping up to
be the fourth or fifth one since her first hospitalization two years
prior, and I couldn't bear it.

I closed my eyes and envisioned myself throwing rocks at the sky,
cursing God for afflicting her with this much suffering. Convinced
that God wasn't caring for her, I knew it was entirely up to me.

In the summer of 2005, her neurologist prescribed weekly inter-
feron injections—a common treatment for patients with her initial
diagnosis of multiple sclerosis.

"I'll bring you an orange and a syringe so you can practice," said
the nurse.

Ayesha fanned her face rapidly, nervously. All I could do was
chuckle and say, "I'll do it."

"You will? You'll give me a shot every week? Oh my God . . . "
Her incredulous expression was priceless. More fanning.

Unfortunately, the shots didn't help and she suffered yet another
exacerbation soon thereafter. Her close friend Erin Googled Ayesha's symptoms and came across a reference to a rare condition:
Devic's disease. Ayesha's neurologist responded skeptically but referred us to the head of neurology at UCSF. "The god of neurology,"
he was one of the few specialists in the country who had experience
with the disease.

Although this was great news, I was terrified of what he might tell us. Devic's—also known as neuromyelitis optica (NMO)—is a horrible disease, attacking the spinal and optic nerves and debilitating the patient through paralysis and blindness. At the time of our visit, patients rarely survived more than eight years after their first onset. It was now August 2005, almost three years after Ayesha's first onset. If indeed she had Devic's, the odds were that she would be dead within the next five years.

The specialist told us that the Mayo Clinic had developed a blood test that could conclusively determine if a patient had Devic's. Ayesha's test came back positive.

Death was no longer a remote possibility; it was inevitable. I began emotionally bracing for it; wondering when and how it would happen, envisioning the ceremonial bathing of her body and the burial, imagining the void that would devour my soul in her absence.

Staving off Devic's was a losing proposition. It was only a matter of time until inflammations and lesions occurred in the upper spinal region—the region that controls critical bodily functions like breathing—and then we would start having conversations about life support and living wills.

And thus began my emotional metamorphosis. The husband and lover receded as the comforter and caregiver emerged. Being *in love* with Ayesha with that fiery newlywed passion seemed unimaginable, because that aspect of love is largely self-serving and self-pleasing. I needed to dedicate the entirety of my emotional reserves to supporting her through a series of progressively aggressive exacerbations and medical procedures that were often frightening and occasionally dangerous.

Instead of dinners, parties, or dancing, our late nights in the city were spent lying side by side in a hospital bed. Sometimes we watched a movie on my laptop, but most often we talked as I massaged her legs while encouraging her to push and pull her feet, rebuilding muscle and regaining strength following bouts of paralysis. I'd bring in decent food to break the monotony of hospital cuisine. These were days of great tenderness; being cooped up in hospital rooms afforded us the time and opportunity to deepen our relationship and truly become family.

One of my favorite activities was reading aloud to her while she rested. We were partway through *The Lord of the Rings* when we learned about a clinical trial for Devic's patients. After a year in which she was hospitalized half a dozen times and her exacerbations appeared to be increasing in ferocity, we were ready to try anything.

We had the incredible fortune to live less than two miles from one of only two places in the world the clinical trial was being offered. Although not everyone responded positively to the treatment, during the two-year study, Ayesha had no exacerbations. This was nothing short of a miracle.

After the trial, we continued the annual treatment schedule. Our only hospital visits were for routine blood tests and protocol follow-ups. I used to think it was trite when people said things like, "At least you have your health." Not anymore.

With minimal exception, the next four years went smoothly, and the specter of death slowly receded. Ayesha was better, I started a new job, our finances stabilized, and we began to live again. It was a relief not to wonder when the next attack was coming. While she wasn't cured, a few years of sustained health earned my faith in the treatment.

The next few years were our happiest yet: we resumed our long walks across town along random streets just to see where they went; we dined out; were plugged into a thriving, diverse Muslim social scene; and made regular trips up to Lake Tahoe. For all intents and purposes, this was our real honeymoon period, years after we first got married.

Which is why, in January 2008, when Ayesha broached the subject of trying to have a child, my immediate response was a mixture of shock and incredulity.

Ayesha required treatment every fifteen months; it couldn't be delayed without risk of relapse. Her treatment consisted of a chemotherapy infusion that could not be used on pregnant women. In addition, the medicine had to have three months to clear her system before we could try to get pregnant.

Attempting to have children seemed reckless after our hard-won reprieve from death. Just the thought of it triggered an emotional backslide; once again she was fragile in my eyes, a patient in recovery, and I was her protector . . . not her lover.

My fear was consuming; if Ayesha became permanently debilitated or worse because we opted to try to have a baby, I would never forgive myself. After all we'd been through early in our marriage and after all the suffering she had endured due to Devic's, there was no fucking way I was putting her well-being at risk.

We talked it through, and decided that we'd wait until the following year and discuss it again, as we were too late in the current treatment cycle to do anything about it. I hoped she'd forget about it. She didn't.

The next year, I reiterated my concerns. Her neurologist—an outstanding doctor whom I trust completely—informed us that women with autoimmune conditions often have symptom-free pregnancies.

I was still terrified.

"I want to say this now, because I don't want it to be an issue later," I said.

She nodded and waited for me to continue.

"If we do this, and your health comes into question, YOU come first. I don't care how far along we are, if there ever comes a time where we have to make a choice to protect you or our unborn child, we protect you. We didn't go through *all that* to put your life back on the line."

"Okay" she said, as she held my hands.

"I don't want to swap you for a baby. I won't. I'll be alone with a baby that I'll resent for no fault of its own, but because it represents a selfish, reckless decision. That's how I'll feel. I'm not even sure that I want a child, but I know that I need you."

She held me and reminded me that we had struggled through the past several years precisely so that we could live our lives, and we ought to do so to the fullest.

Her courage and hope inspired me to take the biggest leap of faith in my life.

In some ways, I was totally prepared for the pregnancy. Compared to the years of Devic's exacerbations, this was a piece of cake. Nausea? No problem. Aches and pains? Sleepless nights? Temperature fluctuations? A walk in the park. Even the unplanned C-section didn't rattle me; I was so used to being in the hospital to fend off illness that being there to bring forth life was a welcome change.

Ayesha was nervous, but I was at her side assuring her that the C-section was going just fine. Then one of the nurses tapped my shoulder and pointed in the direction of the surgeons. I stood slack-jawed as they lifted our baby from her abdomen.

"It's a boy," said the surgeon.

While Ayesha was being closed up in the operating room, I sat with him in the nursery—skin on skin—rocking slowly back and forth. Having this baby was the most optimistic and hopeful act of our lives.

I had never loved so fiercely and uncompromisingly in my life; our son had me wrapped around his tiny fingers. My heart felt as if it had grown three sizes, and I had the strength of ten Randys, plus two. Although my religious adherence was pushed to the brink with Ayesha's illness, I felt a spiritual connection like never before: feeding, loving, protecting, guiding, and teaching this little person who was wholly dependent on me. This provided the ultimate metaphor for my relationship with God. I felt blessed.

And then, doubly blessed. For years, I loved Ayesha as a guardian, caregiver, provider. I needed that persona to cope with her pain and suffering and my fear of losing her. That persona defined me and my love. Being a parent reminded me what it was like to love without baggage, without boundaries. With Ayesha back on a routine treatment schedule with no postpartum complications, I lowered my guard, put aside the caregiver, and became her husband again.

I don't recall the specific day or time, but the sensation was unforgettable. I looked at her and saw my wife—my beautiful, vivacious, inspiring, sexy wife. I felt a love coupled with yearning that I hadn't experienced since those magical days when the workday was a minor purgatory to be endured until I could see her again in the evenings.

Nearly a dozen years later, my professional travels and late afternoons in the office once again are filled with an eagerness to be home.

Glossary

abu (also, abbu or abba): Father.

adaab: A respectful gesture of greeting.

al-Fatiha: The first chapter of the Qur'an, literally "The Opening."

alhamdulillah: An expression of gratitude, literally "Praise be to God."

ammi (also, amma): Mother.

Api: Respectful address for an elder sister or elder female relative.

asr: Daily late-afternoon ritual prayer.

Assalaamu Alaykum/Salaam: Colloquially, "Hello"; literally, "Peace be upon you"/"peace."

ayah: Verse of the Qur'an; a sign of God.

baba: Father.

beta: Daughter or son; also used as a term of endearment.

bhai: Brother.

bilkul: Absolutely.

biryani: Pakistani/Indian rice dish made with spices, meat, and/or vegetables.

Bismillah Al-Rahman Al-Rahim (also, *bismillah*): "In the Name of God, the Compassionate, the Merciful"; the first line of the Qur'an, often used as an invocation of blessing on people, events, and actions.

budha bhais: Old men.

Bukhari and Muslim: A collection of Prophetic sayings or traditions.

chacha: Uncle, specifically the younger brother of one's father.

chokri: Girl.

chulo: Stovetop, gas range.

daal: Lentils.

dars: Religious lesson.

deen: Way of life or faith.

dhikr: A devotional act, typically involving the recitation—mostly silently—of prayers.

dholki: Celebration leading up to a wedding in which the bride and her female family and friends sing and dance to the accompaniment of the *dholak*, a small, two-sided drum.

dua: Personal supplication to God.

dunya: Temporal world.

dupatta: A long scarf.

Eid (also, *Eid-al-fitr*): Muslim holiday that marks the end of Ramadan, the month of fasting.

fajr: Daily, predawn ritual prayer.

fiqh: Islamic jurisprudence.

fitra: Disposition or nature.

gharara: A pair of wide-legged pants with a tunic and scarf worn by women in the Indian subcontinent.

ghotok: matchmaker.

habibi (also, *habibti*): Sweetheart; a term of endearment.

hadith: A saying of the Prophet Muhammad.

halal: Religiously permissible.

halaqa: Religious study circle.

Hanafi: One of the four schools of law in jurisprudence within Sunni Islam.

haram: Religiously proscribed.

hijab: Headscarf.

hijabi: Colloquially, a woman who wears a headscarf.

iftar: Meal to break fast during Ramadan.

iman: Faith.

inshAllah: "God willing."

isha: Daily nighttime ritual prayer.

jaan (also, *jaanu*): Darling; a term of endearment.

jamat khana: Place of worship for *Ismail'i* Muslims.

Jumma: Friday congregational prayer at the mosque.

khaddar: A coarse, homespun cotton cloth.

khoobi: "Good" or "nice."

Khuda hafiz: Colloquially, "good-bye"; literally, "May God be your Guardian," a parting phrase.

khutbah: Religious sermon.

kibbeh: An Arab dish made of bulgur or rice and chopped meat.

kulfi: Ice cream eaten on the Indian subcontinent, often including rosewater and pistachios.

lehnga: A long skirt worn under a top and scarf, worn by women on the Indian subcontinent.

lungi: Sarong.

mahram: A person to whom you are unmarriageable because of blood ties.

mashAllah: Expression of appreciation, joy, praise, or thankfulness for an event or person just mentioned; literally, "As God wills."

masjid: Mosque; a Muslim house of worship.

masoor ki daal: Orange lentils.

maulvi sahib: Colloquially, any bearded, religious man; literally, a religious scholar who is trained to teach people how to read the Qur'an in Arabic.

meem, hah, dal: Letters of the Arabic alphabet (M-H-D) used to spell "Muhammad."

memsahib: Colloquially, a fair-skinned woman; originally referred to British women in colonial India.

mehndi: Henna; also a celebration generally held the night before a wedding in which the bride and her female family and friends are adorned with henna, and everyone feasts, sings, and dances.

mubarak: Blessed; may also be used as a congratulatory term.

mukhabarat: Spies or informants; vice squad.

munnu: Little one; a term of endearment for a young child.

murid: A person who pledges to follow and learn from a spiritual scholar.

naan: Leavened bread baked in a clay oven.

namaaz: One of the five ritual daily prayers, or additional prayers.

Navroz: A festival on the first day of spring, the new year of the Persian calendar. Literally, "new day."

nikah: Islamic legal marriage ceremony.

pakoras: Pieces of vegetable or meat dipped in a spiced batter and deep fried.

rakat: One complete cycle of the ritual prayer.

Ramadan: Sacred month of fasting. The ninth month of the Muslim year, during which strict fasting is observed from sunrise to sunset.

rishta: Marriage proposal.

roti: Unleavened bread, made from stone-ground wholemeal flour.

sabr: Patience.

Sahabah: Companions of the Prophet Muhammad.

salat: One of the five ritual daily prayers, or additional prayers.

sari: A strip of unstitched cloth, worn by women, that is draped over the body.

shaatir: "Smart"; colloquially, "good boy."

shadi: Wedding.

Shaban: The eighth month of the Islamic calendar, preceding Ramadan.

shahada: Declaration of faith.

sham-e-ghazal: An evening of classical poetry recitation, often set to music.

shariah: "Way" or "path"; code of conduct or body of Islamic law.

sheikh: Honorific title; Islamic scholar.

sirat: Path.

sirat al-Mustaqim: "The straight path."

subhanAllah: "Glory be to God"; expression of gratitude or praise upon seeing or hearing something beautiful.

sura (also, *surat*): A chapter of the Qur'an.

Sura al-Fatiha: The opening chapter of the Qur'an.

tabla: A pair of small, attached hand drums, used in South Asian music.

tarawih: Supererogatory congregational night prayers during Ramadan.

tasbih: Prayer beads.

taqwa: God consciousness.

tawhid: Oneness of God.

thobes: Ankle-length garment, usually with long sleeves, like a robe; worn by men in the Middle East and in East Africa.

umma: Family, community, or global Muslim community.

wali: Legal guardian or representative.

wallah: A person involved in some kind of activity, e.g., a chai wallah would be a person who makes and sells chai.

wudu: Ablution before prayer.

Ya Ali madad: A supplication for help by calling on a revered Islamic figure or saint; literally, "Help me, O Ali!"

yalla: "Let's go" or "hurry up."

zina: Sexual intercourse outside of marriage.

Acknowledgments

All praise and gratitude begin with the Most Loving and Most Beautiful.

Thank you to our families—without your love & support this book would not and could not exist.

Our wonderful agent, Ayesha Pande, and literary fairy godparents, David Henry Sterry and Arielle Eckstut—you are our guiding lights.

Laura Mazer, for her mentorship and belief in both of our anthologies.

Our fabulous editor, Amy Caldwell, and the Beacon Press team for being a pleasure to work with from that very first *salaam*.

Deonna Kelli Sayed, for stepping in with such grace and vision.

The *Love, InshAllah* writers, for bravely lighting the way for others to follow.

Our dear columnists and guest writers from around the world, who have deepened the conversation at LoveInshAllah.com.

VONA/Voices, the San Francisco Writers' Grotto, and our writing groups—you are havens in which we craft words, connect, and dream.

And, of course, to all of the men who joined us on this journey with courage, wit, and vulnerability. Thank you.

Contributors

Arsalan Ahmed (pen name) likes maps, poetry, lost causes, and the films of Satyajit Ray. He lives in Virginia.

Ahmed Ali Akbar is a graduate student in Islamic studies. He writes about race, class, South Asian and American Muslim history, and the notion of Islam as a vehicle for social justice. He enjoys dreaming about writing comedy, learning to play music, eight-bit punk rock, color, language, comic books, exploring his family history, and cooking.

Ibrahim Al-Marashi is assistant professor of Middle Eastern history at California State University, San Marcos. He obtained his PhD at the University of Oxford, United Kingdom, completing a thesis on the 1990–1991 Gulf Crisis, part of which was plagiarized by the British government prior to the 2003 Iraq War, otherwise known as the "Dodgy Dossier." He is currently writing a memoir on his experiences as an Iraqi American during America's wars with Iraq. He is also the older brother of Huda Al-Marashi, author of the piece "Otherwise Engaged" in *Love InshAllah: The Secret Love Lives of American Muslim Women.*

John Austin is African American/Japanese American. He converted to Islam fifteen years ago. He is a graduate of George Mason University and runs a small interactive design company in the Washington, DC, area. When not designing, he writes fiction and essays. "Planet Zero" is his first foray into nonfiction.

Alykhan Boolani grew up in Berkeley, California. He was a high school history teacher in nearby Oakland for five years before his recent move to Brooklyn, New York, to help found a new school. He loves being a schoolteacher, and never ceases to be inspired by youth, with their uncanny abilities to resist dogma and mindfully labor toward their own truths—all with love and resilience. When not in the classroom, you can find Alykhan writing short stories, listening to Coltrane, or riding motorcycles with caution.

Arif Choudhury is a writer, filmmaker, stand-up comic, and professional storyteller. In his storytelling program, entitled "More in Common than You Think," Arif shares stories about growing up Bangladeshi American Muslim in the north suburbs of Chicago and pokes fun at issues of ethnic and religious identity, assimilation, and how we think of one another. He wrote a children's book, *The Only Brown-Skinned Boy in the Neighborhood*, and his short film, *Coloring*, is currently being presented in various film festivals. He lives in New York City.

Mohamed Djellouli (pen name) is a wanderer who, one day while lost in the desert, stumbled upon a collection of blessed pens. He has since served as their steward through ink drawings, calligraphy, and poetry. Djellouli's works join the seasonal streams of love and nature. When he is not drawing water for his fellow traveler, he is dancing or practicing law.

Ramy Eletreby is a theater practitioner, facilitator, artist, and activist. He was born in Los Angeles as the third and youngest child of Egyptian parents. Ramy is committed to using theater as a tool for community dialogue and change. He holds an MA in applied theatre from the City University of New York's School of Professional Studies. Ramy has collaborated on community-engaged theater projects both domestically, in California and New York, and internationally, in Africa and the Middle East. Ramy has worked in prisons, schools, places of worship, riverbanks, forests, and other magical places where one would not expect to find theater.

Alan Howard is an IT operations manager with a Fortune 100 Silicon Valley company. He resides in Atlanta with his son, where he enjoys mountain biking, hiking, kayaking, and reading. He is an avid traveler and loves finding new and out-of-the-way places to visit around the world.

Khizer Husain runs Shifa Consulting, a global health consulting practice with a focus on health-care planning, policy, and finance in the Middle East and South Asia. He is also the president of American Muslim Health Professionals. As a 2013–2014 Education Pioneer Fellow, Khizer will provide consulting support to some of the nation's lowest-performing schools in the Washington, DC, area. Khizer writes Muslim-themed children's stories for the iPad app company FarFaria. He attended the London School of Hygiene and Tropical Medicine as a Fulbright Scholar and holds degrees from the University of Illinois, Urbana-Champaign. Khizer lives in Alexandria, Virginia, with his wife, Zuleqa.

A. Khan is completing a graduate degree in religious studies at Harvard University. He is interested in aesthetics, Islamic social history, theories of well-being, ethics, and the lived experiences that bring religious ideals into practice. He is grateful to all his family, past and present, for building an enduring community of love, and to his friends and teachers, past and present, who have helped him become a fuller person. He next plans to pursue some combination of clinical and research training. Long-term, he hopes to continue to be able to write while pursuing his passion for global health and travel. He has lived in the United States, Europe, the Middle East, and North Africa.

Stephen Leeper is a writer-activist and middle school English and social studies teacher living in Oakland, California, with his wife. He graduated from the University of North Carolina at Greensboro with a BA in psychology. Currently he is an MFA candidate in writing at the California College of the Arts. His primary genres are poetry and creative nonfiction.

Haroon Moghul's 2006 novel, *The Order of Light* (Penguin), anticipated the Arab Spring; in it, a young Arab immolates himself and sparks a Middle Eastern revolution. He's been published in *Boston Review*, *Al-Jazeera*, and *Salon*. In 2015, Yale University Press will publish his memoir, *How to Be Muslim*. Haroon has served as an expert guide to Andalucía, Istanbul, and Bosnia, sits on the board of the Multicultural Audience Development Initiative at New York's Metropolitan Museum of Art and is a senior correspondent for *Religion Dispatches*. He is a PhD candidate at Columbia University and was a fellow at the New America Foundation's National Security Studies Program.

Randy Nasson is not a *New York Times* best-selling author but will be one step closer if you purchase this book. Originally from the Boston area, Randy is a software product manager based in San Francisco, where he lives with his wife and son.

Zain Omar grew up in Leicester, England, and San Diego, California. He studied management science at the University of California, San Diego, and currently works in the online marketing industry in Los Angeles. In his free time, Zain likes to spend time with his lovely wife, play soccer (both on the PlayStation and in real life), and hang out with friends and family.

Dan I. Oversaw (pen name) is a Boston-based doctor of religious studies and pop-culture scholar whose wonderful family nevertheless cherishes their privacy. He writes both academic and creative works across a variety of media, lectures nationally on the engagement of pop culture and religion, and teaches throughout the Greater Boston area. The atomic Reform Jewish family of his childhood now also includes Catholics, Presbyterians, Mennonites, agnostics, atheists, and, of course, Muslims—all of whom get along dandily. In cryptological circles, "Dan" made a name for himself by decoding the *Iliad*.

Sam Pierstorff received his MFA in creative writing from California State University, Long Beach. He went on to become the youngest poet laureate ever appointed in the state of California when he was selected to the position in 2004 by the City of Modesto. He currently teaches English at Modesto Junior College. His debut poetry collection, *Growing Up in Someone Else's Shoes*, was published by World Parade Books in 2010, and most recently, he edited *More Than Soil, More Than Sky: The Modesto Poets*, which reached number 1 on Amazon's poetry best-seller's list upon its release.

Yusef Ramelize is a New York City–based activist and graphic designer. He is the founder of HomelessForOneWeek.com, an initiative he began in 2009 to raise awareness about the homeless epidemic in New York City. He has raised over $10,000 for organizations that provide services for the homeless. In 2011, Manhattan borough president Scott Stringer proclaimed him an Artist and Activist against Homelessness. Born in Brooklyn, New York, he currently resides in the Bronx with his wife of two years.

Maher Reham (pen name) is a poet and an applications developer.

Mohammed Samir Shamma was born in 1972 to an Egyptian father and an American mother from Lamesa, Texas. His father died when he was nine and his mother raised him and his younger brother in Houston. Mohammed holds a master of arts degree in Middle Eastern studies from the University of Texas, Austin, and a master of information management and systems degree from the University of California, Berkeley. During the day, Mohammed writes code intended for computers, but at night, after his two kids, Kareem and Leila, are asleep, he writes and illustrates stories. His work is at www.interlinearist.com.

Anthony Springer Jr. is a freelance writer, communications professional, and questioner of everything. He received his bachelor's and master's degrees in Journalism and Media Studies from the University of Nevada, Las Vegas. His work has appeared on Hip HopDX.com, BET.com, TheWellVersed.com, and Arena.com, in *Ultimate MMA* magazine, and elsewhere. He currently blogs about anything and everything on his mind at MrSpringer.wordpress.com. He can be found on Twitter in a never-ending quest for intelligent dialogue @SimplyAnthony.

Yousef "Dr. Yo-Yo" Turshani is an assistant clinical professor of pediatrics at the University of California, San Francisco. He and his wife, Nadeah Vali, Esq., continue their journey together. After Nadeah's time at The Hague, she joined Yousef in Zimbabwe on their first anniversary. They currently reside in Micronesia on the island of Saipan, where they work with the underserved, scuba dive, cook, and pray together. They have couch-surfed in Japan, Indonesia, Malaysia, and Singapore and now open their home to travelers.

EVE RIVERA PHOTOGRAPHY

About the Editors

Editors Ayesha Mattu and Nura Maznavi's first book, *Love, Insh-Allah: The Secret Love Lives of American Muslim Women*, was featured globally by media including the *New York Times*, National Public Radio, the BBC, *Washington Post*, *Guardian*, *Times of India*, *Dawn* (Pakistan), and *Jakarta Post*.

Ayesha Mattu (right) is a writer, editor, and international development consultant. She has worked in the field of women's human rights since 1998. She was selected a Muslim Leader of Tomorrow by the UN Alliance of Civilizations and has served on the boards of IDEX, the Women's Funding Network, and World Pulse. Ayesha is an alumna of the Voices of Our Nations writers' workshop and a member of the San Francisco Writers' Grotto.

Nura Maznavi is an attorney, writer, and Fulbright scholar. She has worked with migrant workers in Sri Lanka, on behalf of prisoners in California, and with a national legal advocacy organization leading a program to end racial and religious profiling. She lives in Chicago.

Follow the writers of *Love, InshAllah* and *Salaam, Love* at
@LoveinshAllah
http://loveinshallah.com/
https://www.facebook.com/LoveInshAllah

Selected one of our anthologies for your book club? Find reading guides on our website and e-mail us at info@loveinshAllah.com to schedule a call or Skype session!